Sociopath

Keys to helping people with aspd

(Recovery from codependent and abusive relationships with sociopaths)

William Coffey

Published By **Cathy Nedrow**

William Coffey

*Sociopath: Keys to helping people with aspd
(Recovery from codependent and abusive
relationships with sociopaths)*

ISBN   978-0-9952066-7-0

Table Of Contents

No part of this guidebook shall be reproduced in any form without permission in writing from the publisher except in the case of brief quotations embodied in critical articles or reviews.

Legal & Disclaimer

The information contained in this book is not designed to replace or take the place of any form of medicine or professional medical advice. The information in this book has been provided for educational & entertainment purposes only.

The information contained in this book has been compiled from sources deemed reliable, and it is accurate to the best of the Author's knowledge; however, the Author cannot guarantee its accuracy and validity and cannot be held liable for any errors or omissions. Changes are periodically made to this book. You must consult your doctor or get professional medical advice before using any of the suggested remedies, techniques, or information in this book.

Chapter 1: The Case Of Ted Bundy

A. Brief Overview of Ted Bundy's Crimes

Ted Bundy, born Theodore Robert Bundy, modified into an American serial killer, kidnapper, rapist, and necrophile who terrorized more youthful girls at a few diploma in the 1970s. Bundy is understood to have murdered as a minimum 30 ladies at some point of multiple states, despite the fact that the proper variety of his sufferers may be better. His unpleasant crimes concerned abducting women, sexually assaulting them, and then brutally killing them. Bundy's potential to persuade smooth of seize for good-bye may be in component attributed to his attraction, intelligence, and seemingly regular appearance. His case garnered sizeable interest from the media, and he in the end acquired 3 loss of life sentences for his crimes. Bundy changed into finished in the electric powered powered chair on January 24, 1989, at Florida State Prison.

B. Demonstrating the Traits of Psychopathy and Sociopathy in Bundy's Behavior

Ted Bundy exhibited severa tendencies related to each psychopathy and sociopathy, which made his case particularly thrilling to researchers and the overall public alike. Some of these dispositions encompass:

Charm and Manipulation: Bundy modified into appeared for his charisma and functionality to govern the ones spherical him. He regularly used his attraction to lure his sufferers proper into a faux sense of safety in advance than abducting and killing them. Bundy have become moreover able to preserve a reputedly regular life, keeping down jobs or even attending law university, whilst concurrently committing his heinous crimes.

Lack of Empathy and Remorse: Bundy displayed a whole lack of empathy for his patients and their families, regularly engaging in cruel and sadistic behavior. He exhibited no remorse for his movements, even going up to now as to taunt the authorities and the households of his sufferers with data of his crimes.

Narcissism and Grandiosity: Bundy exhibited narcissistic tendencies, along with a grandiose sense of self-importance and a notion that he have become above the law. He often represented himself in court docket docket docket, showcasing his conceitedness and perception in his private intelligence.

Impulsivity and Risk-taking: Bundy established impulsivity and hazard-taking behaviors at some point of his criminal profession. He frequently targeted sufferers in public places and completed his crimes in volatile conditions, which consist of abducting girls from crowded regions or breaking into their houses on the equal time as they slept.

Antisocial Behavior: Bundy's criminal conduct escalated through the years, starting with robbery and voyeurism and culminating within the brutal murders of numerous younger girls. This sample of increasingly violent and delinquent behavior is regular with the tendencies of psychopathy and sociopathy.

C. The Impact of Bundy's Case on Public Awareness and Understanding of Psychopathy and Sociopathy

Ted Bundy's case had a profound impact on public interest and records of psychopathy and sociopathy. His apparently ordinary appearance and functionality to mixture into society shattered the stereotype of the "excellent" serial killer and forced humans to confront the reality that psychopaths and sociopaths can be located amongst us.

Bundy's case moreover highlighted the importance of know-how the dispositions and behaviors associated with psychopathy and sociopathy, as this know-how can assist to find out capability risks in our groups. In the years because of the truth that Bundy's arrest and execution, his case has been significantly studied via psychologists, criminologists, and different specialists, supplying precious insights into the minds of psychopaths and sociopaths.

The notoriety of Bundy's case has moreover added on extended public hobby in actual crime testimonies, in addition to a fascination with the darker additives of human nature. This heightened consciousness has sparked important conversations about intellectual fitness, crook justice, and the prevention of violent crime.

Defining Psychopathy and Sociopathy

A. Historical Perspectives on Psychopathy and Sociopathy

The requirements of psychopathy and sociopathy have advanced through the years, with roots in early studies of deviant behavior and intellectual contamination. The term "psychopathy" have become first brought by using the use of German psychiatrist Julius Koch inside the past due nineteenth century to describe a person sickness characterized with the aid of immoral conduct and a lack of empathy [5]. On the alternative hand, the time period "sociopathy" emerged inside the early twentieth century as an alternative descriptor for humans displaying delinquent behavior and a dismiss for societal norms [4]. Over time, each phrases were used interchangeably, no matter the reality that differences were made in more current studies and diagnostic standards [6].

B. Key Differences Between Psychopaths and Sociopaths

While there can be significant overlap in the tendencies exhibited via psychopaths and sociopaths, some key variations can be diagnosed. For instance, psychopaths frequently display greater calculated and manipulative behaviors, at the same time as sociopaths will be predisposed to be extra impulsive and erratic of their moves [8]. Additionally, psychopaths can be able to maintain a semblance of normalcy of their lives, together with retaining down a technique or forming relationships, while sociopaths regularly struggle to accomplish that due to their antisocial behaviors [9]. However, it's far vital to be aware that those variations aren't absolute, and man or woman times may present various combos of tendencies associated with every psychopathy and sociopathy.

C. The Role of Biology, Genetics, and Environment

Research shows that every genetic and environmental factors play a function inside the development of psychopathy and sociopathy [2]. From a organic attitude, studies have recognized structural and practical variations in the brains of human beings with psychopathic tendencies, mainly in regions related to empathy, impulse manage, and emotional processing [3]. Genetic factors may additionally furthermore make a contribution to the development of these character problems, with some evidence suggesting a heritable component to psychopathy and sociopathy [2].

Environmental impacts, which include childhood abuse or forget, can have interaction with those genetic and natural predispositions, probably exacerbating the development of psychopathic and sociopathic traits [2].

D. The Spectrum of Psychopathy and Sociopathy

Both psychopathy and sociopathy can be understood as current on a spectrum, with individuals showing numerous tiers of tendencies related to these character disorders. The Diagnostic and Statistical Manual of Mental Disorders (DSM) presently categorizes psychopathy and sociopathy under the wider analysis of Antisocial Personality Disorder (ASPD) [6]. However, it's miles crucial to apprehend the unique traits and manifestations of each sickness, as they could have one-of-a-kind implications for remedy and control.

Chapter 2: Neurodevelopment Perspective

Some researchers recommend that the neurobiological abnormalities decided in psychopaths may be the result of neurodevelopmental disruptions [9]. This angle indicates that the structural and purposeful mind variations located in psychopaths are not static, however as an alternative can also evolve over time due to genetic, environmental, and epigenetic factors. The psychopathic brain is characterised with the aid of structural and useful abnormalities in key mind regions.

Early signs and signs and symptoms of psychopathy

Elaborating at the early signs and symptoms and signs and signs and symptoms of psychopathy, it's miles crucial to recognize that those signs and symptoms can seem in a distinctive manner in every body. However, a few commonplace early signs and symptoms and symptoms may be found all through several domains, collectively with emotional, interpersonal, and behavioral components.

Callous-unemotional tendencies: Children or children with psychopathic dispositions may additionally show off a lack of empathy and feature problem expertise the emotions and emotions of others. They can also show insensitivity to the struggling or misery of others and feature a restricted potential for guilt, regret, or remorse for his or her actions.

Conduct issues: Early signs and symptoms and signs and symptoms of psychopathy may additionally consist of persistent and excessive rule-breaking behavior, deceitfulness, and manipulation. These human beings might also moreover engage in theft, destruction of property, or acts of aggression and violence, which encompass bullying or physical altercations.

Narcissism: Narcissistic trends in people with psychopathic inclinations may additionally moreover arise as an inflated experience of self-worth, excessive self-hobby, and a want for admiration or hobby from others. They can also show a revel in of entitlement and push aside the dreams or feelings of others.

Impulsivity: Impulsive behaviour is every other early signal of psychopathy. These human beings may moreover have difficulty controlling their impulses, task risky or risky activities with out considering the capability outcomes of their actions. They may additionally moreover war with planning and forethought, leading to negative choice-making and reckless behaviour.

Irresponsibility: A sample of irresponsibility may be an early sign of psychopathy. These people may moreover have problems keeping extended-term goals or commitments, which embody academic or occupational hobbies, and can regularly have interaction in irresponsible behavior, inclusive of no longer lovely duties or over and over conducting sports that can reason damage to themselves or others.

Shallow feelings: Children or children with psychopathic tendencies may also additionally furthermore display shallow or superficial feelings. They also can have trouble forming actual emotional connections with others, and their emotional expressions also can seem insincere or contrived.

Lack of fear or inhibition: Early signs of psychopathy can also additionally encompass a discounted revel in of worry or anxiety in conditions in which maximum human beings may additionally commonly enjoy such emotions. This can result in reckless or dangerous behaviour, as the individual won't certainly understand or renowned the functionality effects of their actions.

It is critical to apprehend that the presence of one or extra early symptoms and signs and symptoms does not continually suggest that an character will boom psychopathy. The development of psychopathy is complex and includes the interaction of genetic, environmental, and social factors. Early identification of those symptoms can assist in offering suitable manual and intervention to mitigate the effect of those elements at the individual's existence.

Socio-Cultural Factors Favouring the Development of Psychopathy

Cultural norms and values

Cultural norms and values play an critical feature in shaping individual conduct and social interactions [1]. Cultures that promote aggression, violence, or the recognition of antisocial conduct may also moreover moreover create an environment that encourages or tolerates psychopathic developments. On the alternative hand, cultures that price empathy, cooperation, and prosocial conduct may additionally moreover discourage the improvement of psychopathy.

Social inequality and poverty

Social inequality and poverty can make a contribution to psychopathology with the resource of growing disturbing dwelling situations and proscribing get right of get admission to to to belongings vital for wholesome development [2]. Children and young adults growing up in impoverished or deprived environments may be greater prone to growing psychopathic developments due to the dearth of opportunities for great increase, social manual, and schooling.

Family and parenting styles

Family dynamics and parenting styles play a essential feature in shaping the development of psychopathy. Parental psychopathology, substance abuse, and a loss of warmth, responsive parenting can boom the danger of growing psychopathic inclinations in youngsters [3]. Inconsistent or harsh location might also make contributions to the improvement of these dispositions.

Peer impacts

Negative peer impacts can make contributions to the development of psychopathy, as youngsters or young folks who companion with deviant friends can be more likely to interact in antisocial behavior and increase psychopathic traits [4]. Peer strain, bullying, and social isolation can also play a feature in shaping psychopathic dispositions.

Media and technology

The effect of media and era at the improvement of psychopathy is a place of growing problem. Exposure to violent or aggressive content material fabric in tv, movies, video video video games, or social media may additionally moreover make contributions to the development of psychopathic inclinations by means of using normalizing violence and desensitizing humans to the suffering of others [5].

Understanding the socio-cultural elements that preference the improvement of psychopathy is essential for growing powerful prevention and intervention techniques. By addressing those elements, it could be viable to reduce the prevalence of psychopathy and sell more healthful social environments for people and businesses. Further studies is needed to find out the complicated interplay of socio-cultural factors and psychopathy, similarly to the improvement of targeted interventions aimed within the route of mitigating those influences.

Real-Life Examples and Case Studies

1. Culture and Values: The "Code of the Street" Subculture

In his ebook "Code of the Street," sociologist Elijah Anderson describes a manner of life in a few city areas of the USA wherein avenue violence and aggression are valued as a method of survival and gaining understand [7]. This manner of life, which regularly exists in economically deprived neighborhoods, promotes a set of norms and values that can inspire the development of psychopathic inclinations in folks who stay inside the ones businesses.

2. Social Inequality: The Cycle of Poverty and Psychopathy

The case of Robert Hare's "Without Conscience" highlights how the cycle of poverty and psychopathy can perpetuate itself. In the ebook, Hare describes a more youthful guy who grew up in a extensively disadvantaged environment, experiencing abuse, overlook, and poverty [5]. As a end result, he advanced psychopathic tendencies, which further extended his probability of carrying out criminal and antisocial behaviors, perpetuating a cycle of social drawback and psychopathy.

3. Family and Parenting Styles: The Impact of Child Abuse

The case of Mary Bell, a British female who killed more youthful boys on the age of eleven, demonstrates the capability effect of own family dynamics and parenting patterns on the development of psychopathy. Bell skilled severe abuse, neglect, and a pretty dysfunctional circle of relatives environment, all of which contributed to her developing psychopathic traits and appealing in immoderate acts of violence [5].

4. Peer Influences: The "Psychopath Magnet" Effect

A examine with the useful resource of way of Dishion, Patterson, and pals [4] observed that youngsters who associated with deviant pals were more likely to boom psychopathic tendencies. This phenomenon, referred to as the "psychopath magnet" effect, happens whilst people with psychopathic developments are interested in each unique and make stronger their delinquent behaviours. The case of Eric Harris and Dylan Klebold, the perpetrators of the 1999 Columbine High School taking photographs, is an instance of the capability effect of lousy peer impacts on the improvement of psychopathy.

five. Media and Technology: The "Slender Man" Stabbing Case

The 2014 "Slender Man" stabbing case highlights the capability have an effect on of media and technology at the development of psychopathy. Two 12-yr-antique girls, Anissa Weier and Morgan Geyser, lured their friend into the woods and stabbed her 19 times in an try and please the fictitious individual "Slender Man," whom that that they had observed about through on line boards and videos [5]. This case demonstrates how publicity to violent content material at the net can make contributions to the improvement of psychopathic dispositions and violent behaviour in younger people.

Prevention and early intervention strategies for Psychopath

Prevention and early intervention strategies for psychopathy are essential to restrict the impact of this example on individuals and society. Addressing the danger factors associated with psychopathy can help reduce the probability of its improvement and sell more healthy, greater empathetic conduct. Some key strategies embody:

Early identification: Regular checks and screenings, specifically in at-danger populations, can assist come to be aware about those who can be growing psychopathic trends. Early identity lets in well timed interventions and help for every the character and their families.

Parenting training and useful resource: Providing assets, training, and aid to parents can promote wholesome and regular parenting practices, which may additionally assist reduce the chance of developing psychopathic traits in children. Encouraging first rate determine-toddler relationships, establishing easy boundaries, and selling emotional law are vital additives of powerful parenting.

Chapter 3: The Sociopathic Mind

The sociopathic thoughts is characterised through a totally precise and complicated array of tendencies and behaviors that make it difficult for those affected to shape emotional attachments, show erratic and unpredictable behaviors, and display delinquent character dispositions. Sociopaths are liable to anger, aggression, social deviance, and rule-breaking. This economic smash dreams to find out those tendencies in element and talk their capability effect on both the individual and society.

A. Difficulty Forming Emotional Attachments:

Sociopaths frequently warfare to shape deep emotional connections with others. They may additionally additionally have hassle empathizing with the feelings and feelings of those round them, that might make it tough for them to set up and keep meaningful relationships [2]. This lack of emotional attachment can result in superficial connections and a dismiss for the desires and properly-being of others.

B. Erratic and Unpredictable Behaviors:

Sociopaths are regarded for their impulsive and erratic conduct patterns, which can seem in various strategies. They may also moreover regularly change jobs or relationships, have problem making lengthy-time period commitments, and interact in reckless or risky sports [4]. Their unpredictable nature can make it tough for others to accept as real with them and might create instability of their private and professional lives.

C. Antisocial Personality Traits:

Individuals with a sociopathic mind regularly show off delinquent personality tendencies, collectively with a persistent pattern of dismiss for the rights and emotions of others. They might also additionally forget about approximately social norms and criminal guidelines, lie, deceive, and manage others for private advantage or pride [1].

Additionally, they may show a experience of superiority and be tremendously opinionated [1].

D. Prone to Anger and Aggression:

Sociopaths are vulnerable to anger and aggression, often suffering to manipulate their feelings. This can bring about not unusual conflicts with others and an elevated danger of assignment violent or terrible behaviors [6]. Their lack of ability to manipulate their anger successfully can in addition exacerbate their delinquent inclinations and contribute to their social isolation.

E. Social Deviance and Rule-Breaking:

Sociopaths regularly have interaction in social deviance and rule-breaking behaviors, at the facet of crook hobby, substance abuse, and one-of-a-kind kinds of misconduct [2]. Their willingness to interact within the ones actions is regularly pushed thru their loss of empathy and issue for the results in their moves, further to their choice for personal advantage and strength [9].

The sociopathic thoughts offers a very particular set of annoying conditions for each the man or woman and society. Understanding the inclinations and behaviors related to this person type can help clinicians, own family individuals, and buddies better assist and manage people with sociopathic inclinations. While treatment alternatives for sociopathy are constrained, early intervention and suitable useful resource can enhance the high-quality of life for those suffering from this complicated and often misunderstood situation.

Early Signs of Sociopathy and Factors Causing Sociopathy

Sociopathy, a time period frequently used interchangeably with Antisocial Personality Disorder (ASPD), is characterized with the resource of a pattern of brush aside for the rights and feelings of others. Identifying early signs and signs of sociopathy can be crucial in imparting suitable interventions and help. It is equally critical to recognize the factors that contribute to the improvement of sociopathy so one can better deal with its reasons and mitigate its impact on humans and society.

Early Signs of Sociopathy:

Persistent mendacity or deceit: Sociopaths often engage in ordinary mendacity or deception, even if there may be no obvious gain to doing so [2].

Manipulation of others: Sociopaths generally tend to apply enchantment, wit, or intelligence to manipulate others for personal benefit or pride [1].

Lack of empathy: A wonderful sign of sociopathy is a loss of empathy, making it difficult for human beings to recognize or relate to the feelings and emotions of others [7].

Violation of social norms and policies: Sociopaths frequently brush aside social norms, felony hints, and policies, regularly important to social deviance and rule-breaking behaviors [2].

Aggressive conduct: Sociopaths might also moreover furthermore show competitive behavior and have problem controlling their anger [6].

Irresponsibility: They frequently conflict with fulfilling private, expert, or economic responsibilities, demonstrating a pattern of irresponsibility [1].

Impulsivity: Sociopaths are liable to impulsive preference-making, critical to erratic and unpredictable behaviors [4].

Factors Causing Sociopathy:

Genetics: Research suggests that genetic elements can also make contributions to the development of sociopathy. There is proof that a predisposition to delinquent conduct can be inherited [3].

Environmental impacts: Adverse kids stories, collectively with exposure to violence, abuse, or overlook approximately, also can boom the risk of developing sociopathic inclinations [3].

Parenting: Inconsistent, neglectful, or harsh parenting styles can make contributions to the improvement of antisocial behaviors and sociopathic inclinations in kids [3].

Brain abnormalities: Studies have found that humans with sociopathy can also moreover furthermore show off structural and beneficial abnormalities within the mind, particularly in areas accountable for empathy, impulse manage, and moral reasoning [10].

Recognizing early signs of sociopathy and knowledge its contributing factors can facilitate early intervention and useful useful resource for the ones affected. A entire approach to addressing sociopathy must involve a aggregate of genetic, environmental, and social factors at the way to increase powerful prevention and remedy techniques.

Prevention and early intervention techniques for Sociopathy:

1.   Parenting schooling: Providing property and aid to mother and father so you can promote healthy and constant parenting practices can help reduce the threat of developing sociopathic traits in kids.

2.   Early identity: Identifying at-danger youngsters and teens via everyday tests and screenings can permit well timed interventions and help for every the person and their households.

three. Mental health help: Providing get right of entry to to intellectual fitness services for children and young human beings who've professional trauma, abuse, or overlook also can additionally assist mitigate the development of sociopathic dispositions.

4.   Social skills training: Teaching kids and youngsters powerful verbal exchange, empathy, and battle decision competencies can assist in fostering healthy social

relationships and lowering antisocial behaviors.

Treatment for individuals with sociopathic dispositions may moreover incorporate:

1. Psychotherapy: Various therapeutic techniques, which includes cognitive-behavioral treatment (CBT), can be employed to help people apprehend the results in their movements, growth empathy, and study extra adaptive approaches of managing stressors.

2. Medication: Although there are not any unique medicinal drugs for sociopathy, sure medicinal tablets may be prescribed to deal with co-happening conditions which incorporates anxiety, depression, or impulsivity.

3. Support agencies: Participation in aid corporations can offer individuals with a secure area to percentage their research and study from others who are managing similar challenges.

4.   Structured programs: In a few times, more extensive interventions, at the side of residential remedy programs or recovery groups, may be beneficial for humans with excessive sociopathic dispositions.

In stop, know-how the early signs and symptoms of sociopathy and the factors that make a contribution to its improvement is vital that lets in you to offer appropriate prevention, intervention, and remedy strategies. By addressing the genetic, environmental, and social factors associated with sociopathy, we are able to better guide the ones affected and promote extra healthful, greater empathetic, and socially accountable behavior in our businesses.

Fictional Character Moriarty from Sherlock Holmes as Psychopath and Sociopath

Professor James Moriarty, a fictional man or woman created via Sir Arthur Conan Doyle in the Sherlock Holmes memories, is often regarded for instance of every a psychopath and a sociopath. As the "Napoleon of Crime,"

Moriarty is a criminal mastermind and Holmes' arch-nemesis. Let's take a look at some of his dispositions which may be indicative of psychopathy and sociopathy:

Psychopathic Traits:

Superficial appeal: Moriarty is quite sensible and can be pretty captivating even as important. He makes use of this enchantment to manipulate others and similarly his crook desires.

Lack of empathy: Moriarty is cold and calculating, with little to no regard for the emotions or properly-being of others. He is inclined to commit heinous crimes with none visible regret.

Grandiose revel in of self confidence: Moriarty sees himself as a genius and advanced to others, which include Holmes. This self-aggrandizing view drives him to interact in complex and immoderate-stakes crook sports activities.

Impulsivity and need for stimulation: Moriarty thrives on the pleasure of crook interest and the venture of outsmarting Holmes. He takes dangers and constantly seeks new tactics to venture himself and check his mind.

Sociopathic Traits:

Deceitfulness: Moriarty is a hold close of deception and manipulation, the usage of lies and foxy to attain his dreams. He regularly constructs elaborate schemes to dedicate crimes and keep away from seize.

Antisocial conduct: Moriarty displays a sample of crook conduct that disregards the rights and safety of others. He shows no regret for his moves and feels no duty to paste to societal norms or criminal hints.

Chapter 4: The Characters Of Shakespeare

Shakespeare's performs have featured characters that exhibit tendencies of psychopathy and sociopathy, frequently serving as compelling antagonists. Here are some high-quality examples:

Iago (Othello): Iago is taken into consideration without a doubt considered one of Shakespeare's maximum notorious villains, characterised thru his deceitfulness, manipulation, and lack of empathy. As a psychopath, Iago shows superficial attraction, cunning intelligence, and a chilly-hearted nature. He manipulates Othello and others to gain his desires, inflicting chaos and tragedy without regret.

Richard III (Richard III): Richard III is a conniving and ruthless person who well-knownshows traits of each psychopathy and sociopathy. As a psychopath, he demonstrates a grandiose revel in of self-worth, manipulativeness, and shortage of empathy. As a sociopath, he indicates an utter dismiss for social norms, undertaking a ruthless pursuit of strength with out a problem for the properly-being of others.

Lady Macbeth (Macbeth): Lady Macbeth is an example of someone who suggests some psychopathic dispositions, especially her loss of empathy and manipulative nature. She is pushed with the resource of ambition and is willing to visit immoderate lengths to assist her husband gather strength, in spite of the reality that it way orchestrating murder. Lady Macbeth's cold-hearted nature and push aside for the lives of others make her a compelling and chilling man or woman.

Aaron (Titus Andronicus): Aaron, a cunning and ruthless man or woman in Titus Andronicus, shows trends of every psychopathy and sociopathy. He is pushed with the aid of a choice for revenge and has no qualms approximately causing harm to others, even orchestrating the rape and mutilation of a younger woman. Aaron's lack of empathy, deceitfulness, and violent inclinations make him a risky and memorable antagonist.

Edmund (King Lear): Edmund, the illegitimate son of Gloucester in King Lear, is a foxy and ambitious person who indicates sociopathic tendencies. He manipulates his own family and others to further his non-public hobbies, betraying his father and brother within the approach. Edmund's deceitful nature, lack of empathy, and push aside for social norms make him a compelling villain.

These Shakespearean characters showcase unique components of psychopathy and sociopathy, contributing to the complexity and intensity of the testimonies wherein they seem. Their actions and motivations offer insight into the darker side of human nature, making them charming figures within the realm of literature.

Psychopathy and Sociopathy inside the characters of Dostoevsky

Fyodor Dostoevsky's novels frequently delve into the complexities of human nature, with severa characters showing tendencies of psychopathy and sociopathy. Here are a few brilliant examples:

Raskolnikov (Crime and Punishment): Raskolnikov, the protagonist of Crime and Punishment, may be taken into consideration a sociopath. He rationalizes his desire to dedicate murder with a principle that positive top notch people have the right to transgress moral limitations for the extra appropriate. Raskolnikov's movements, alongside collectively collectively with his brush aside for social norms and his loss of remorse to begin with, illustrate sociopathic dispositions.

Svidrigailov (Crime and Punishment): Svidrigailov is a man or woman who shows psychopathic developments, in conjunction with a lack of empathy, manipulative conduct, and a records of immoral and crook acts. His pursuit of more youthful ladies and indifference to the suffering of others make him a risky and unsettling presence in the novel.

Ivan Karamazov (The Brothers Karamazov): Ivan, one of the three brothers in The Brothers Karamazov, reveals a few sociopathic tendencies, especially his highbrow detachment from moral norms and empathy. Ivan's philosophical mind, inclusive of his rejection of God and his notion in the absence of regular moral values, contribute to the unfolding tragedy within the novel.

Smerdyakov (The Brothers Karamazov): Smerdyakov, the illegitimate son of Fyodor Karamazov, is someone who shows trends of each psychopathy and sociopathy. He is manipulative, deceitful, and demonstrates a loss of empathy for others. Smerdyakov's moves are pushed via his resentment inside the route of his own family and society, culminating in a heinous crime that impacts the lives of the Karamazov brothers.

Stavrogin (Demons): Stavrogin, a essential character in Demons, famous psychopathic tendencies, which encompass a lack of empathy, impulsiveness, and a records of violent and immoral behavior. He is worried in severa criminal and detrimental sports activities and exerts a powerful have an impact on over the opportunity characters, essential them down a dark path.

Dostoevsky's characters regularly grapple with moral dilemmas and existential questions, and those who showcase psychopathic or sociopathic tendencies provide a window into the darker elements of human nature. These complicated, multi-dimensional characters allow Dostoevsky to find out problem topics together with guilt, redemption, and the results of immoral movements.

Psychopathy and Sociopathy in the characters of infamous Gangsters, Drug Smugglers and Mafia bosses

Psychopathy and sociopathy are generally related to individuals who have interaction in criminal sports which incorporates drug smuggling, organized crime, and mafia sports activities. In this financial ruin, we will discover the traits of psychopathy and sociopathy within the characters of notorious gangsters, drug smugglers, and mafia bosses, through actual-lifestyles case studies.

Case Study 1: Pablo Escobar

Pablo Escobar emerge as a notorious Colombian drug lord who rose to energy in the 1970s and 1980s, and became one of the wealthiest guys in the global through his cocaine smuggling sports. Escobar exhibited the various trends related to psychopathy, along with a loss of empathy and a push aside for social norms and regulations. He changed into regarded for his ruthless techniques, which blanketed bribery, violence, and homicide.

Escobar additionally exhibited a sample of instability and chaos, each in his personal lifestyles and in his criminal sports activities. He had a statistics of impulsive and reckless behavior, and engaged in manipulative methods to get what he desired. Despite his many crimes and atrocities, Escobar have end up frequently seen as a charismatic discern with the useful resource of those around him, the use of his enchantment and air of mystery to govern and manage others.

Case Study 2: John Gotti

John Gotti changed into a notorious American mafia boss who rose to strength within the Eighties and Nineteen Nineties. Gotti exhibited some of the tendencies associated with sociopathy, which includes a loss of empathy and a brush aside for social norms and policies. He modified into stated for his ruthless techniques, which covered violence and murder, and had a reputation for being a "Teflon Don" because of his ability to stay far from prosecution.

Gotti moreover exhibited a sample of manipulative conduct, the usage of his appeal and air of mystery to manipulate and control others. He changed into seemed for his extravagant life-style, which protected luxurious cars, apparel, and jewelry. Despite his crook sports activities, Gotti grow to be often seen as a charismatic determine with the beneficial useful resource of those around him, the use of his appeal and air of thriller to hold his energy and feature an effect on.

Case Study three: Joaquin "El Chapo" Guzman

Joaquin "El Chapo" Guzman became a notorious Mexican drug lord who rose to energy in the Eighties and Nineties. Guzman exhibited some of the tendencies related to psychopathy, collectively with a lack of empathy and a brush aside for social norms and recommendations. He turned into mentioned for his ruthless techniques, which protected violence and murder, and feature emerge as one of the wealthiest guys within the global through his drug smuggling activities.

Guzman additionally exhibited a sample of manipulative conduct, using his attraction and air of mystery to maintain his power and effect. He had a statistics of impulsive and reckless conduct, and engaged in manipulative techniques to get what he desired. Despite his many crimes and atrocities, Guzman modified into often visible as a charismatic decide with the aid of those round him, using his attraction and air of mystery to govern and manipulate others.

The case studies supplied above highlight the developments of psychopathy and sociopathy inside the characters of notorious gangsters, drug smugglers, and mafia bosses. These humans exhibited a pattern of instability and chaos, assignment impulsive and reckless behavior, and the usage of manipulative strategies to get what they preferred. Despite their many crimes and atrocities, they have been often visible as charismatic figures with the aid of those round them, using their appeal and air of mystery to maintain their electricity and effect. Understanding the trends of psychopathy and sociopathy is essential for spotting the warning signs and symptoms of unstable human beings and shielding yourself from their impact.

Psychopathy and Sociopathy within the characters of politicians and dictators

Psychopathy and sociopathy are not constrained to criminals or people in the underworld. These tendencies moreover may be observed in a few politicians and dictators. Here are a few actual-life case research of politicians and dictators who exhibited trends of psychopathy and sociopathy.

Politicians:

Adolf Hitler - Hitler changed into the chief of Nazi Germany and answerable for the deaths of loads of hundreds of human beings inside the direction of World War II. He exhibited many developments related to psychopathy, together with a lack of empathy, manipulative conduct, and a disregard for social norms and regulations.

Joseph Stalin - Stalin end up the chief of the Soviet Union and chargeable for the deaths of loads of lots of people at some stage in his regime. He exhibited many traits associated with sociopathy, in conjunction with a loss of empathy, manipulative behavior, and a dismiss for social norms and rules.

Richard Nixon - Nixon have turn out to be the thirty 7th President of america and resigned from workplace due to his involvement inside the Watergate scandal. He exhibited many developments related to psychopathy, which includes a loss of empathy, manipulative conduct, and a dismiss for social norms and guidelines.

Idi Amin - Amin was the President of Uganda and responsible for the deaths of hundreds of masses of humans in the course of his regime. He exhibited many tendencies related to sociopathy, such as a lack of empathy, manipulative conduct, and a push aside for social norms and guidelines.

Chapter 5: The Psychopath's Charm And Manipulation Tactics

Psychopaths are diagnosed for his or her ability to enchantment and manipulate others to get what they need. Their loss of empathy and judgment of proper and incorrect makes them adept at exploiting the vulnerabilities in their targets. This economic catastrophe will discover the psychopath's appeal and manipulation strategies, providing perception into how they operate and a manner to guard yourself from their affect.

The Charm Offensive

Psychopaths are regularly able to enchantment their dreams successfully, using their herbal air of secrecy and social skills to win humans over. They are professional at studying people and identifying their weaknesses, tailoring their approach to healthful anyone. Psychopaths may additionally moreover additionally use flattery, compliments, and offers to assemble rapport and benefit the hold in mind of their targets.

One of the simplest techniques utilized by psychopaths is "love bombing," in which they shower their goals with affection, interest, and items. This immoderate and overwhelming show of love could make the cause experience unique and valued, developing a enjoy of dependence on the psychopath. This can be especially effective in romantic relationships, where the psychopath may additionally moreover use love bombing to speedy installation a deep emotional connection.

Manipulation Tactics

Once the psychopath has won the don't forget and dependence of their goal, they'll begin to manipulate them to obtain their dreams. Psychopaths are expert at identifying the dreams and goals in their dreams, and will use this comprehend-a way to control them. They might also moreover use guilt, shame, or fear to govern their goals, regularly making them revel in accountable for the psychopath's properly-being.

Gaslighting is each different not unusual tactic utilized by psychopaths, wherein they manage their goal's perception of fact. They also can deny or distort activities, or use selective reminiscence to make their target doubt their personal reminiscences or perceptions. This should make the goal enjoy pressured and uncertain, and might reason them to more susceptible to the psychopath's have an impact on.

Psychopaths also can use isolation as a tactic to control their goals. They can also discourage their intention from spending time with buddies or circle of relatives, or even sabotage their relationships. This can create a sense of dependence on the psychopath and make the purpose greater susceptible to their effect.

Protecting Yourself

The exceptional way to shield your self from the enchantment and manipulation strategies of a psychopath is to be aware of the caution symptoms and symptoms. If someone seems too ideal to be proper, or if you experience uncomfortable or uneasy spherical them, it's far critical to pay attention in your instincts. Trustworthy human beings do no longer want to constantly flatter or control others to win their agree with.

Recognize pink flags in relationships: The first step in retaining off poisonous relationships is to be aware about the warning symptoms. This includes behaviors which includes manipulation, mendacity, impulsiveness, instability, and emotional abuse. By spotting those crimson flags early on, you can take steps to shield your self and avoid getting further worried in a poisonous relationship.

Trust your instinct: In each of the case research, the humans had a intestine feeling that some thing became incorrect of their relationship. Trusting your instinct is an crucial part of recognizing crimson flags and defensive your self from poisonous relationships. If a few detail feels off or uncomfortable, it's far crucial to take a step returned and evaluate the scenario.

Establish smooth barriers: Setting obstacles is important in any relationship, however especially in toxic ones. Boundaries help you keep your experience of self and shield your self from being manipulated or taken gain of. It's crucial to speak your barriers definitely and stand organisation in implementing them.

Prioritize your private properly-being: In each of the case studies, the human beings in the end recognized the importance of prioritizing their very personal nicely-being. This approach spotting at the same time as a relationship isn't serving you and taking steps to stop it, although it feels difficult or uncomfortable. Ultimately, your very own fitness and happiness need to be your top precedence in any courting.

Psychopaths are professional at captivating and manipulating others, the use of their natural aura and shortage of empathy to take benefit of the vulnerabilities of their dreams. Understanding the psychopath's techniques and being aware of the caution symptoms and signs will will let you guard your self from their have an effect on. By setting up easy boundaries, surrounding yourself with supportive human beings, and prioritizing self-care, you can build resilience and keep your enjoy of self within the face of a psychopath's appeal and manipulation.

Recognizing Sociopathic pattern

Sociopaths are individuals who lack empathy and function a brush aside for social norms and regulations. They often interact in impulsive and irresponsible behaviors and function trouble forming large relationships. In this chapter, we're able to discover the sociopath's sample of instability and chaos, providing belief into a way to apprehend the caution symptoms and signs of sociopathy and a way to shield yourself from their have an impact on.

Impulsivity and Recklessness

Sociopaths are acknowledged for his or her impulsivity and reckless behaviour. They might also furthermore engage in unstable activities along with substance abuse, volatile riding, or promiscuity with out situation for the consequences. They also can furthermore have a information of impulsive behaviour, at the side of stealing or mendacity, and can lack a enjoy of guilt or regret for their actions.

Chaotic Relationships

Sociopaths regularly have hassle forming and keeping full-size relationships. They may also have a information of short-lived or tumultuous relationships and might battle to set up emotional connections with others. Sociopaths can also engage in manipulative behaviour in their relationships, which incorporates lying, dishonest, or the use of others for his or her very very personal advantage.

Manipulative Behaviour

Sociopaths may use manipulative techniques to get what they need, which includes enchantment, flattery, or deception. They can be adept at reading others and identifying their weaknesses, using this information to their benefit. Sociopaths might also additionally furthermore engage in gaslighting, wherein they control others' notion of truth at the manner to govern them.

Lack of Responsibility

Sociopaths regularly lack a experience of responsibility for his or her movements and their effect on others. They also can additionally blame others for his or her issues or refuse to take duty for his or her mistakes. They may also additionally have a statistics of quitting jobs or forsaking responsibilities.

Protecting Yourself

The quality manner to protect your self from the have an impact on of a sociopath is to be aware of the caution signs and symptoms. If someone exhibits a pattern of impulsive, reckless, or manipulative behaviour, it's critical to take a step back and examine the situation. Trustworthy individuals take duty for their actions and do now not interact in manipulative or risky behaviour.

It's also vital to establish clean barriers and stand organization in imposing them. Don't permit yourself to be manipulated or taken gain of through a sociopath. Surround your self with supportive pals and circle of relatives who can provide a truth take a look at and assist you hold your experience of self.

Finally, are looking for help in case you enjoy like you're in a risky or abusive scenario. There are sources available for those who need assist, together with hotlines and counselling services.

Recovering from relationships with psychopaths and sociopaths

A. Recovering from relationships with psychopaths and sociopaths.

Recovering from a relationship with a psychopath or sociopath can be a tough and stressful approach. It's essential to are seeking out expert help if you are struggling to cope with the aftermath of the shape of relationship. Some coping techniques for enhancing from those relationships embody:

Seeking therapy or counseling to paintings via the trauma and rebuild your enjoy of self confidence.

Engaging in self-care sports sports, collectively with exercising, mindfulness, and meditation, to reduce stress and sell emotional recuperation.

Creating a assist community of trusted buddies and family those who can offer emotional manual and a secure location to machine your emotions.

Practicing forgiveness and letting flow of negative feelings towards your abuser, which permit you to pass on and reputation on your personal recovery.

B. Building emotional resilience and self-care

Building emotional resilience and practicing self-care assist you to amplify the internal power and resources to navigate hard situations and relationships. Some strategies for building emotional resilience encompass:

Building a first-class attitude through gratitude, mindfulness, and powerful affirmations.

Engaging in everyday exercising, that might help reduce pressure and sell emotional nicely-being.

Maintaining a wholesome food regimen and getting sufficient sleep, which could help decorate ordinary bodily and emotional health.

Practicing self-compassion and self-popularity, which let you domesticate a greater powerful courting with your self.

C. Learning from beyond reviews

Learning from beyond memories permit you to increase and increase as someone, and permit you to avoid making the same errors inside the destiny. Some techniques for studying from beyond studies embody:

Reflecting on past relationships and evaluations to find out styles and regions for boom.

Seeking comments from trusted friends and circle of relatives individuals to gain new perspectives and insights.

Engaging in self-reflected photograph and journaling to way your mind and emotions and gain a deeper understanding of your self.

D. Fostering wholesome relationships and social connections

Fostering healthy relationships and social connections will will can help you construct a strong guide community and cultivate a revel in of belonging and connection. Some techniques for fostering wholesome relationships consist of:

Building a strong community of pals and circle of relatives folks who can provide emotional assist and a revel in of network.

Engaging in sports sports and pastimes that carry you pride and let you meet new humans.

Volunteering or turning into a member of network agencies, which will let you connect to like-minded people and make a outstanding effect for your network.

Chapter 6: Confronting The Reality Of A Sociopathic Relationship

The hassle of managing a sociopathic partner isn't always one which may be effects unnoticed or dismissed. Many those who locate themselves in a courting with a sociopath are regularly blind to their companion's actual nature at the begin They may be drawn in through way of their attraction, aura, and capability to control, pleasant to later find out the actual amount in their deceit and shortage of empathy.

The effects of being in a dating with a sociopath may be devastating. The ordinary lies, manipulation, and emotional abuse can leave someone feeling pressured, annoying, and isolated. They can also query their very own sanity and war to don't forget their very own perceptions.

The hassle is similarly complex thru the usage of the reality that sociopaths are frequently particularly professional at masking their tracks and hiding their right nature. As M.E.

Thomas writes in her e-book "Confessions of a Sociopath," "We cover in easy sight, unmasking ourselves to those we accept as true with, and then slipping silently once more into the shadows, commonly on shield."

This capacity to mixture in and mimic everyday feelings is what unit's sociopaths other than psychopaths. While psychopaths are effects diagnosed as cold and remorseless, sociopaths can regularly seem captivating, exquisite, or even loving. But beneath this façade lies a person without a ethical compass, no ability for empathy, and no revel in of obligation for their movements.

One of the important thing annoying situations in managing a sociopathic companion is the lack of beneficial useful resource and data from others. Unlike handling a more visible form of abuse, consisting of physical or verbal, emotional abuse from a sociopathic companion is regularly invisible to the ones at the outdoor. Friends and circle of relatives may not understand the depths of manipulation and deceit that stand up in the back of closed doorways, leaving the sufferer feeling remoted and by myself.

Compounding this isolation is the truth that many people in sociopathic relationships have unknowingly come to be enmeshed in their accomplice's net of lies. The sociopath may moreover have remoted their associate from their guide device, making it tough for them to searching for help or manual. Additionally, the sufferer may additionally warfare with feelings of disgrace and embarrassment for being in a dating with a sociopath, in addition stopping them from assignment out for help.

Another mission in coping with a sociopathic partner is the regular cycle of gaslighting and manipulation. Gaslighting is a form of highbrow abuse wherein the abuser seeks to make their sufferer doubt their very very own truth. They may also moreover twist and distort sports, deny their movements, or shift the blame onto the victim. This steady manipulation can leave the victim feeling pressured and doubting their non-public perceptions of reality.

Furthermore, sociopaths are also recognised for his or her lack of duty and their functionality to shift blame onto others. This could make it hard for their sufferers to hold them answerable for their moves, and can additionally contribute to a experience of powerlessness and frustration.

In the primary 1/2 of of this ebook, we are capable of find out the hassle of coping in a sociopathic courting in more intensity. We will speak the developments of sociopaths and the manner they differ from different sorts of abusers. We may additionally even delve into the precise demanding situations and obstacles that patients of sociopathic abuse face, from isolation and gaslighting to the lack of guide and duty.

By expertise the problem handy and the particular stressful conditions it gives, we are capable of start to make bigger strategies for coping and restoration from this kind of toxic dating. While there may be no clean answer, there is preference for those who have positioned themselves entangled with a sociopathic companion. Together, we're capable of navigate the complexities of sociopathic relationships and start the adventure inside the direction of reclaiming our lives.Breezy and witty, presenting personal anecdotes and insights from the writer's very very own experience.

As I sit down down all of the manner down to write this chapter, I can not help but sense a moderate twinge of tension. After all, the mission we're approximately to dive into isn't always an smooth one. It's a hassle that many humans face, but few are inclined to overtly speak. It's a mission which could go away us feeling burdened, trapped, and powerless. It's the hassle of being in a sociopathic courting.

Now, earlier than we move any in addition, permit's outline what precisely a sociopathic courting is. In clean terms, it is a relationship wherein one or each companions show off sociopathic trends or behaviors. These can encompass a loss of empathy, manipulative inclinations, impulsivity, and a brush aside for the emotions and properly-being of others. And on the same time as this may sound like an incredible prevalence, the truth is that sociopathic relationships are greater common than we anticipate.

Think about it – have you ever ever ever been in a dating in which you constantly felt such as you have been walking on eggshells? Where you located your self continuously questioning your own sanity and instincts? Where your partner seemed to have a totally considered certainly one of a kind set of values and morals? If so, you could have been in a sociopathic courting with out even figuring out it.

But why is that this problem so important to deal with? Why can't we in reality brush it under the rug and flow into on with our lives? Well, the reality is that being in a sociopathic relationship may additionally have damaging consequences on our intellectual and emotional well-being. It can leave us feeling worn-out, isolated, and stripped of our self confidence. It also can lead us to impeach our very personal judgment and ability to form healthful relationships inside the destiny.

I apprehend all too well the impact that a sociopathic relationship may additionally have on someone. As the writer of "Confessions of a Sociopath: A Life Spent Hiding in Plain Sight," I actually have lived via my sincere share of those types of relationships. And allow me permit you to understand, they will be now not easy to navigate. They are like a workout of chess, with the sociopathic associate constantly changing the regulations and manipulating the final effects to their advantage.

But what makes those relationships even extra complicated is the truth that sociopaths are experts at camouflage. They understand precisely a way to mixture in and appear charming and charismatic at the floor. This makes it fantastically difficult to choose out them or maybe extra hard to leave the relationship as fast as we recognise who they genuinely are.

So, now that we recognize the trouble, what can we do approximately it? Well, the first step is spotting that we're in a sociopathic dating. This may be a tough and painful popularity, however it's miles crucial if you want to float ahead. From there, we're capable of begin to educate ourselves on sociopathy and its results on relationships.

But likely the most critical thing we are able to do is to attend to ourselves. In a sociopathic relationship, we regularly overlook about approximately our very personal wishes and nicely-being a great way to delight our accomplice. But this simplest perpetuates the cycle of manipulation and manipulate. By prioritizing our very very very own emotional and highbrow health, we're able to begin to interrupt free from the poisonous grip of a sociopathic accomplice.

It's additionally crucial to bear in mind that we are not on my own. Sociopathic relationships are extra common than we count on, and there are various property available to help us cope and heal. Whether it is treatment, manual corporations, or absolutely talking to a depended on buddy or member of the family, we ought not to face this mission by myself.

In the give up, being in a sociopathic dating isn't always a reflected image of our well worth or individual. It is a give up end result of being focused via someone with a manipulative and antisocial character. But through teaching ourselves and searching after our nicely-being, we will smash free from the draw near of a sociopathic associate and flow into within the course of a happier and healthier future.

Chapter 7: Thriving In A Sociopathic Relationship

As a sociopath, I honestly have spent my lifestyles navigating through relationships with a completely particular mind-set. I am in a regular united states of america of reading and manipulating those spherical me, usually in search of the subsequent opportunity to apply a person to my benefit. But as a first rate deal as I enjoy the energy and control that includes being a sociopath, I additionally understand the toll it is able to tackle those at the receiving end of my actions.

This is specifically real almost about intimate relationships. The lack of empathy and push aside for others' feelings that are inherent in sociopathy must make it tough to keep a healthy and appealing partnership. But through my personal studies and observations, I actually have advanced a solution – a way to effectively cope in a sociopathic dating.

The first step in this answer is to understand and well known which you are in a sociopathic relationship. This can also appear obvious, however normally, the insidious nature of sociopathy could make it difficult to pinpoint the suitable problem. You may additionally moreover feel continuously manipulated or emotionally tired, but no longer apprehend why. Being capable of label the connection as sociopathic is vital in being capable of correctly cope.

Once you've got got diagnosed the trouble, the subsequent step is to set obstacles. Sociopaths are notorious for pushing boundaries and crossing strains, so it's far essential to set up clean and company barriers early on in the courting. These limitations need to be non-negotiable and surely communicated. It is also crucial to stick to those obstacles and not allow the sociopath to govern you into compromising them.

Another key thing of coping in a sociopathic courting is retaining your very personal experience of self. Sociopaths have a way of making their companions experience nugatory and dependent on them. It is important to stand as a great deal as this and hold onto your non-public identity and self-worth. This will no longer first-rate help you deal with the sociopath's behavior, however moreover make it less complicated to go away the relationship if critical.

Communication is also essential in a sociopathic dating. It is vital to be direct and honest on your communique, as sociopaths regularly use manipulation and gaslighting strategies to avoid taking duty for their actions. By being direct and no longer letting them deflect or twist the communique, you may keep them chargeable for their conduct.

Self-care is also a essential component of coping in a sociopathic courting. Sociopaths may be draining and emotionally arduous, so it's far crucial to take time for yourself and have interaction in sports activities that bring you happiness and peace. This need to consist of hobbies, spending time with supportive pals and own family, or looking for treatment to device your feelings.

Finally, it is important to apprehend that a sociopathic courting won't be sustainable long-term. While some can be able to manage and cope in the ones relationships, it isn't continuously the healthiest alternative. If you find out that your intellectual and emotional properly-being is usually compromised, it is able to be important to give up the relationship and prioritize your very own self-care.

Coping in a sociopathic dating isn't always smooth, but it's miles feasible. By spotting the problem, setting limitations, retaining your experience of self, speakme correctly, working closer to self-care, and being willing to go away if critical, you may navigate thru this specific and tough dynamic. Remember to prioritize your very own well-being and in no way compromise your barriers for the sake of the relationship.After delving into the complicated and regularly destructive global of sociopathic relationships, it's time to shift our interest to finding an answer. As M.E. Thomas has set up us thru her private critiques in "Confessions of a Sociopath: A Life Spent Hiding in Plain Sight," sociopathic relationships may be quite destructive and difficult to navigate. But there may be desire. By information the individual of sociopathy and using confirmed techniques, it's far viable to manipulate or even thrive in a sociopathic courting.

One of the maximum vital steps in locating a solution is to understand that sociopathy is a persona sickness, not only a behavioral hassle. This manner that the way a sociopath thinks, feels, and behaves is basically precise from that of a neurotypical individual. This distinction is essential because it lets in us to approach the relationship from an area of empathy and records in location of judgment and blame.

The first approach for coping in a sociopathic courting is setting clear limitations. Sociopaths will be inclined to push barriers and check limits, so it's miles crucial to establish and put in force barriers early on. This may be difficult, as sociopaths are expert at manipulating and gaslighting their companions. But with the aid of manner of being organization and regular in our barriers, we're able to save you the sociopath from taking gain mother and father or causing harm.

Another vital approach is self-care. Sociopathic relationships may be emotionally and mentally draining, so it is important to take care of ourselves. This can contain on the lookout for treatment or help companies, locating healthful coping mechanisms, and prioritizing our very personal nicely-being. Self-care moreover includes setting aside time for ourselves and pursuing our very own pursuits and passions, destroy loose the sociopathic partner.

Communication is likewise key in coping with a sociopathic associate. While it is able to be tempting to avoid battle and hard conversations, it's important to deal with problems and concerns as they rise up. However, it's crucial to approach conversation strategically. Sociopaths are skilled at twisting conversations and using gaslighting techniques to manipulate their companions. This is why it's miles crucial to live calm, live with the data, and now not interact in emotional arguments.

In addition to individual strategies, searching for outside help also can be useful in managing a sociopathic dating. This can consist of remedy, assist companies, or perhaps confiding in a depended on friend or member of the family. It's critical to have a help system in location for instances at the same time as we can also feel overwhelmed or need steerage.

Finally, it's vital to understand while a sociopathic dating is now not sustainable.

Despite our terrific efforts, some sociopathic relationships may additionally furthermore certainly be too toxic and bad to maintain. In these times, it's far essential to prioritize our very very own well-being and nicely cast off ourselves from the situation.

However, the solution to coping in a sociopathic relationship may not give up with just person strategies. It's furthermore vital to address societal attitudes and perceptions closer to sociopathy. Too regularly, society stigmatizes and demonizes human beings with sociopathic tendencies, that would make it tough for humans to attempting to find help and useful resource. By advocating for added knowledge and empathy closer to sociopaths, we are able to create a greater inclusive and supportive environment for the ones struggling in sociopathic relationships.

"Living with a Sociopath: Personal Accounts of Surviving Manipulation and Deception"

insightful and uncooked.

Real-Life Example 1: Jane's Marriage to a Sociopath

Jane had met James in university and turn out to be right away inquisitive about his captivating person and air of secrecy. They fell in love and got married quickly after commencement. At first, their marriage regarded fantastic, but as time went on, Jane commenced out to have a look at uncommon behaviors in James.

He must lie about small things, manage her into doing matters she did no longer want to do, and showed a loss of empathy for others. Jane did no longer think a good deal of it inside the beginning, but as their dating advanced, she commenced to revel in like she changed into walking on eggshells around James.

It wasn't until they were married for five years that a mutual friend delivered Jane to the concept of sociopaths. She started out out to investigate and study books like "Confessions of a Sociopath" to better recognize her husband's behavior. As she dove deeper into the concern, she decided out that James healthy the profile flawlessly.

Jane modified into devastated. She loved her husband and couldn't believe that he may be a sociopath. She struggled with the realization that their entire dating may additionally moreover moreover were a lie.

But armed with this new statistics, Jane emerge as able to navigate her marriage in a exceptional manner. She determined the way to defend herself from James' manipulation and a way to set boundaries. Although their marriage become far from excellent, Jane positioned strategies to manage and maintain her very private highbrow properly-being.

Real-Life Example 2: John's Toxic Boss

John had been jogging on the equal company enterprise for 10 years and had constantly acquired rave evaluations for his work. However, while a latest boss, Emily, took over his branch, subjects began to change.

Emily become fascinating and charismatic, but John fast discovered out that she modified into moreover manipulative and cold-hearted. She could in all likelihood take credit score rating score for John's paintings and throw him underneath the bus even as subjects went incorrect. She additionally showed a loss of empathy inside the path of her employees, frequently making harsh and hurtful comments.

John felt trapped in his manner. He wanted the profits and wasn't certain if he also can need to find a new approach with the cutting-edge united states of the undertaking marketplace. He furthermore didn't want to jeopardize his profession via way of speaking out in the direction of his boss.

But after reading "Confessions of a Sociopath," John started out to look his boss in a top notch mild. He realized that Emily displayed many tendencies of a sociopath and that her conduct have become no longer a mirrored picture of his genuinely worth as an worker.

John started to distance himself from Emily and centered on his artwork and his personal intellectual properly-being. He additionally reached out to HR and documented any instances of mistreatment. Eventually, Emily's right nature changed into exposed, and she or he end up permit cross from the company. John turned into able to circulate on from the poisonous art work surroundings and find out a trendy hobby in which he grow to be respected and valued.

Real-Life Example 3: Sarah's Toxic Friendship

Sarah had been buddies with Jen due to the fact that they've been in excessive faculty. They have been thru masses together and had always been there for every other. However, as they were given older, Sarah started out out to look at that Jen displayed some troubling behaviors.

Jen become always the middle of interest and had no hassle mendacity or manipulating others to get what she desired. She moreover confirmed a lack of empathy toward others and may frequently use Sarah's vulnerabilities in competition to her in arguments.

Sarah felt caught within the friendship. She didn't want to lose her kids pal, however she additionally did now not apprehend the manner to manipulate Jen's manipulative and toxic behavior.

But after studying approximately sociopaths in "Confessions of a Sociopath," Sarah commenced out to look her pal in a awesome mild. She realized that Jen's conduct changed into no longer ordinary and that she grow to be now not a exceptional impact on her lifestyles.

Although it modified into difficult, Sarah ended the friendship and focused on surrounding herself with supportive and real pals. It have become a tough selection, however in the end, Sarah end up capable of discover peace and happiness without the steady toxicity of her former buddy.

By analyzing and studying about sociopaths, humans can choose out crimson flags and defend themselves from manipulation and harm. It isn't clean, however with the right gear and useful resource, it's miles viable to hold one's highbrow properly-being and thrive in a sociopathic relationship.Uniquely right to supplying the ones examples because her e-book delves into her non-public studies as a sociopath.

M. E. Thomas stocks numerous actual-lifestyles examples in her book "Confessions of a Sociopath" that shed moderate on coping in a sociopathic relationship. These examples now not simplest offer perception into the mind of a sociopath but moreover provide practical recommendation for individuals who can also find themselves in a similar state of affairs.

One of the most effective examples in the e-book is at the same time as Thomas discusses her marriage to a non-sociopathic guy. Despite her loss of empathy and potential to control others, Thomas decided herself falling in love with this man and ultimately marrying him. However, as she exhibits in the e-book, her sociopathic inclinations finally induced the downfall of their dating.

Through this case, Thomas highlights the difficulties of retaining a relationship with a sociopath and the toll it could take at the non-sociopathic associate. She acknowledges that at the identical time as sociopaths may be charming and capable of satisfy the goals in their partners in the starting, their loss of empathy and manipulation can in the long run lead to the destruction of the connection.

Another example Thomas stocks is her enjoy with law school and the criminal profession. As a sociopath, Thomas located herself excelling in law college, the usage of her charm and manipulation to get in advance. However, she moreover data the toll this profession took on her intellectual fitness and the manner it in addition fueled her sociopathic tendencies.

Through this situation, Thomas highlights the risks of professions that require manipulation and absence of empathy. She moreover offers recommendation for people who may be in comparable professions on the manner to manipulate and maintain their intellectual properly-being.

Thomas moreover shares the story of a chum who became in a dating with a sociopath. This pal, like many others, changed into initially attracted to the sociopath's allure and air of thriller but eventually have end up the sufferer of manipulation and abuse. Through this example, Thomas emphasizes the importance of recognizing pink flags and setting barriers in relationships with sociopaths.

Overall, the actual-life examples shared thru M. E. Thomas in her e-book offer a glimpse into the complexities of coping in a sociopathic dating. They offer valuable insights and realistic advice for those in comparable situations, in addition to a deeper know-how of the thoughts of a sociopath. These examples characteristic a reminder that sociopaths aren't honestly characters in books or movies, however actual people with the potential to purpose harm to the ones spherical them.

"Mastering the Art of Coping: Unveiling the Strategies and Techniques for Surviving a Sociopathic Relationship"

Chapter 8: Strategies And Techniques

Living in a sociopathic dating can be mentally and emotionally hard. The regular manipulation, deceit, and shortage of empathy from a sociopathic accomplice can leave you feeling tired and out of place. However, there are great techniques and techniques that allows you to permit you to cope with the challenges of being in a sociopathic courting. In this financial disaster, we are able to discover these strategies in detail and offer you with a step-through-step manual for enforcing them efficiently.

1. Educate Yourself on Sociopathy

The first step in managing a sociopathic relationship is to train yourself on sociopathy and its trends. Sociopathy is a persona ailment characterised via a lack of empathy, manipulative conduct, and a disregard for social norms. By studying more about this ailment, you can higher understand your companion's behavior and not take it for my part.

2. Set Boundaries

Establishing obstacles is vital in any dating, but it's far specifically critical in a sociopathic one. Sociopaths frequently push barriers and take a look at limits, so it's miles essential to set easy and business organisation obstacles from the start. Communicate your barriers in your accomplice and be consistent in enforcing them. This will assist shield your properly-being and save you your associate from taking benefit of you.

3. Practice Self-Care

Being in a sociopathic dating can take a toll in your intellectual and emotional nicely-being. It is critical to prioritize self-care and cope with yourself throughout this hard time. Make time for sports activities that supply you pleasure, surround your self with supportive friends and own family, and are trying to find treatment or counseling if favored. Remember, you can not cope with others if you aren't searching after your self first.

4. Communicate Effectively

Effective communique is crucial in any relationship, but it's far mainly vital in a sociopathic one. Sociopaths are professional manipulators and frequently twist terms and situations to their advantage. To avoid misunderstandings and gaslighting, be smooth and direct to your conversation. Use "I" statements to specific your feelings and keep away from blaming or accusing your partner.

5. Keep a Journal

Keeping a mag may be a useful coping mechanism in a sociopathic courting. It allows you to record incidents and their consequences on you. Writing down your mind and emotions can also provide a revel in of release and assist you approach your feelings. In addition, a magazine can function proof if you ever need to go away the relationship or take jail motion.

6. Seek Support

Do now not try to deal with a sociopathic courting by myself. Seek guide from depended on pals and own family or be a part of a assist group for humans in comparable conditions. Talking to others who have been through similar reviews can offer validation, records, and encouragement.

7. Practice Detachment

Detachment is a important coping method at the same time as coping with a sociopathic associate. It entails detaching yourself emotionally out of your partner's manipulative strategies and now not taking their behavior for my part. You can workout detachment by using way of the use of placing emotional barriers, reminding yourself of your personal self confidence, and focusing on your personal well-being.

8. Develop an Exit Plan

It is crucial to have a plan in place in case you ever decide to move away the connection. Sociopaths frequently do now not take breakups nicely and may inn to excessive measures to manipulate or manage you to live. Develop a safety plan and are seeking out the assist of a expert if needed to make sure your protection and nicely-being at the same time as leaving the connection.

nine. Focus on Yourself

In a sociopathic dating, it is easy to get caught up in your accomplice's world and lose sight of your personal want and dreams. Make an attempt to recognition on your self and your private private increase. Take up new hobbies, set goals for your self, and invest time and energy in sports activities that supply you pleasure and achievement. This will help you maintain a experience of self and now not lose your self in the relationship.

10. Trust Your Instincts

Lastly, receive as actual with your instincts close to your companion's behavior. If a few factor feels off or does not upload up, it is likely due to your partner's manipulations.

Sociopaths are draw close manipulators, and they will visit tremendous lengths to deceive and manipulate their partners. If your intestine is telling you some trouble is wrong, pay attention to it and take motion.

1. Establish Boundaries:

One of the most critical techniques for coping in a sociopathic courting is to installation and maintain easy obstacles. Sociopaths are regarded for his or her loss of empathy and admire for barriers, so it's miles as much as you to set the ones limits and ensure they will be valid. This also can consist of saying no to their goals or lowering off touch once they start manipulating or abusing you.

2. Do Not Engage in Their Games:

Sociopaths thrive on energy and manipulate, and that they often play mind video video games to mention their dominance over their sufferers. It is crucial to now not fall into their traps and get stuck up of their video video games. Instead, stay calm and rational, and do now not allow their tries to provoke you or make you enjoy responsible have an effect on you.

3. Be Aware of Gaslighting:

Gaslighting is a form of manipulation in which the sociopath attempts to make you doubt your personal sanity or belief of reality. They may additionally moreover twist records, deny sports, or use extraordinary strategies to make you question your non-public reminiscence and judgment. To cope with this, it is vital to stay grounded on your non-public truths and not permit their gaslighting strategies have an effect on you.

four. Build a Support System:

A sociopathic courting may be emotionally draining and retaining apart, so it's crucial to have a strong manual system in area. Reach out to pals and own family for help, and keep in mind becoming a member of a assist institution for people who've been in comparable situations. Having a useful resource tool can offer you with the emotional aid and validation you want to cope with the relationship.

five. Practice Self-Care:

In a poisonous dating, it is simple to lose sight of your very private wishes and nicely-being. However, going for walks towards self-care is important in your mental, emotional, and physical health. This can encompass carrying out pursuits, workout, and taking time for your self to lighten up and recharge. Taking care of your self will assist you maintain your strength and resilience in the face of a sociopathic associate.

6. Educate Yourself:

Knowledge is power, and coaching yourself about sociopathy and manipulative behaviors can provide you with a better expertise of your accomplice's moves and help you deal with them higher. You can read books, attend workshops or counseling intervals, or perhaps talk to a therapist approximately your opinions. Education can also help you understand warning signs and symptoms and protect yourself within the destiny.

7. Seek Professional Help:

If you are struggling to cope with the connection or experiencing emotional or physical abuse, it's far essential to are looking for for expert assist. A therapist or counselor can provide you with the vital support and steering to cope with the toxic dynamics of a sociopathic dating and artwork within the direction of recovery and recuperation.

eight. Prepare for an Exit Strategy:

In a few times, it is able to be important to go away the sociopathic relationship to your very very own safety and nicely-being. It is important to have a nicely-idea-out go out technique in vicinity that takes into consideration any functionality risks and ensures your protection. This may moreover additionally contain looking for the help of a home violence secure haven or concerning law enforcement if desired.

9. Accept Your Feelings:

Being in a sociopathic dating can deliver up numerous emotions, which embody anger, fear, confusion, or even guilt. It is essential to widely diagnosed and take delivery of the ones emotions in choice to suppressing them. They are a legitimate reaction to a toxic scenario, and thru acknowledging and processing them, you can pass towards healing and reclaiming your energy.

10. Trust Your Instincts:

Lastly, constantly trust your instincts. If some element does not enjoy proper in the courting, it probably isn't always. Sociopaths are professional at manipulation and can attempt to make you doubt yourself, however your instincts will guide you in the route of what's nice for you. Pay hobby to crimson flags and listen in your intestine on the identical time as it tells you some aspect is off.

Chapter 9: Navigating The Obstacles Of A Sociopathic Relationship

Introduction: Living in a sociopathic relationship may be as an alternative difficult and unfavorable. You may additionally additionally sense trapped, manipulated, and continuously strolling on eggshells. But you are not on my own. Many humans have been in comparable situations and function located strategies to overcome the barriers that include being in a sociopathic courting. In this financial ruin, we're capable of find out some of the not unusual boundaries that you may come across and offer steering on how to conquer them.

Identifying the Sociopathic Tendencies: One of the most important hurdles in coping with a sociopathic courting is figuring out the sociopathic inclinations in your associate Sociopaths are regarded for their manipulative and captivating nature, making it difficult to apprehend their real intentions They can also control you into questioning that their conduct is ordinary or which you are the trouble. It is vital to educate yourself on the signs and symptoms and signs and symptoms of sociopathic behavior and accept as true with your instincts. Seeking professional assist also can be useful in figuring out and records the sociopathic dispositions in your companion.

Recognizing Your Own Behavior: When in a sociopathic dating, it's miles commonplace to adopt a number of the equal manipulative behaviors as your associate you also can sense the want to lie or manage a good way to protect yourself or keep away from war However, it is crucial to apprehend and damage this cycle of poisonous behavior. Therapy can be a beneficial device in statistics and overcoming the ones learned behaviors.

Setting Boundaries: Sociopaths are infamous for pushing limitations and violating the boundaries of others It is critical to set easy and corporation barriers with your partner. This may moreover furthermore embody speakme your desires and obstacles, and being regular in imposing effects even as the ones boundaries are crossed. It may also be important to set bodily limitations, which incorporates finding a stable region to retreat to at the same time as feeling overwhelmed or threatened.

Dealing with Gaslighting: Gaslighting is a commonplace tactic utilized by sociopaths to manipulate and control their sufferers. It entails manipulating a person into questioning their non-public belief of truth. If you find out your self continuously doubting your own thoughts and emotions, it's far vital to are attempting to find manual from a trusted friend, member of the family, or therapist. They can offer an outdoor mindset and assist you regain self perception for your very non-public perceptions.

Coping with Emotional Abuse: Emotional abuse is a shape of intellectual violence that might have severe consequences for your highbrow and emotional properly-being. Sociopaths may also use emotional abuse as a way to control and control their sufferers. It is essential to understand emotional abuse and are searching out assist from a therapist or assist group. They can offer validation and assist you amplify healthy coping mechanisms.

Finding Support: Coping with a sociopathic courting can be exceptionally putting apart. You may also moreover enjoy like you can not take delivery of as real with all of us, together with family and pals. It is essential to reap out and gather a aid device. This may moreover furthermore encompass remedy, becoming a member of a manual organization, confiding in a depended on buddy, or looking for assist from a domestic violence secure haven. Having a help device can provide validation, steering, and a steady vicinity to precise your emotions.

Leaving the Relationship: Leaving a sociopathic courting can be the maximum difficult obstacle to overcome. You can also have advanced a robust emotional and intellectual attachment on your associate, making it hard to break away. Additionally, sociopaths are identified for his or her manipulative and controlling nature, making it hard to head away the relationship accurately. It is essential to create a protection plan and are searching for guide from a home violence safe haven or hotline earlier than seeking to go away the connection.

Remembering Your Worth: Sociopaths often prey on humans with low vanity and cause them to sense unworthy and powerless. It is crucial to keep in mind your in reality simply really worth and cost as someone. You are not described with the aid of your dating with a sociopath. Practice self-care, surround yourself with supportive humans, and remind yourself which you are well worth of affection and apprehend.

Obstacle 1: Recognizing the Sociopathic Behavior

One of the maximum essential boundaries in a sociopathic courting is spotting the sociopath for who they certainly are. Sociopaths are expert at manipulation and deception, and that they regularly appear captivating and charismatic at the floor. It may be difficult to look beyond their façade and understand that their conduct is not normal or healthy.

Overcoming this impediment starts offevolved with education your self approximately the trends and behaviors of sociopathy. This will let you apprehend the nature of the connection and come to be aware about purple flags. It is also important to don't forget your instincts and no longer dismiss any problems or suspicions you may have. Listening in your intestine can save you from being trapped in a poisonous and perilous dating.

Obstacle 2: Setting Boundaries

Sociopaths will be predisposed to push boundaries and manipulate their partners to get what they want. This can go away the non-sociopathic associate feeling powerless and emotionally tired. Setting barriers is crucial in any relationship, however it becomes even extra critical even as one companion is a sociopath.

Setting boundaries method truly speaking your dreams and expectancies to the sociopath. It furthermore way being enterprise and sticking to the ones barriers, even if the sociopath attempts to push them. It can be hard to confront a sociopath, however fame your ground is crucial in your non-public well-being and to keep a sense of manipulate inside the courting.

Obstacle three: Managing Emotions

Being in a dating with a sociopath can be emotionally taxing. Sociopaths lack empathy and do now not have the functionality to like or take care of their companions the manner a mean person could. As a end end result, the non-sociopathic associate can enjoy extreme feelings, inclusive of anger, frustration, and unhappiness.

One way to conquer this obstacle is to exercising emotional detachment. This does no longer mean shutting down your feelings, but as an alternative gaining knowledge of to understand and renowned them without allowing them to control you. It is also essential to are looking for for help from buddies, family, or a therapist to way your emotions and build a robust guide machine.

Obstacle four: Ending the Relationship

For many human beings, the concept of completing a courting with a sociopath can be daunting. Sociopaths frequently use manipulation and fear tactics to keep their companions from leaving. They may additionally additionally moreover threaten to damage themselves or their partner if the relationship ends. However, staying in a sociopathic relationship can be negative to at least one's intellectual and emotional nicely-being.

To conquer this impediment, it's miles vital to keep in mind that your protection and nicely-being want to normally be your pinnacle precedence. Seek guide from own family and buddies, and do not forget reaching out to a therapist or a home abuse hotline for steering and help in correctly ending the connection.

Obstacle five: Healing and Moving On

Leaving a sociopathic courting does no longer robotically guarantee a luckily-ever-after finishing. In truth, it is not unusual for people to revel in trauma and emotional distress even after the relationship has ended. This is why it's miles vital to prioritize restoration and self-care after leaving a poisonous relationship.

The recuperation approach may include remedy, self-reflected picture, and surrounding your self with great and supportive humans. It is also critical to recognize that it isn't your fault for being in a sociopathic relationship and to forgive your self for any perceived errors or shortcomings.

"Embracing the Truth: A Call to Take Control and Thrive in a Sociopathic Relationship"

As we come to the stop of this e-book, I want to first thanks for becoming a member of me on this journey thru the complexities of sociopathic relationships. It takes courage to confront and explore this shape of difficult challenge rely, and I commend you for taking this step.

Throughout this e-book, we've delved deep into the thoughts of a sociopath and determined out approximately their manipulative methods, lack of empathy, and potential to misinform and enchantment. We have moreover mentioned the devastating outcomes of being in a relationship with a sociopath, from emotional and psychological abuse to financial destroy and physical damage.

But most significantly, we've got explored techniques to manage and protect ourselves from the detrimental impact of those relationships. We have cited the significance of putting limitations, spotting purple flags, and attempting to find assist from cherished ones or experts.

I want that via this ebook, you have got had been given obtained a better know-how of sociopathy and its results on relationships. My purpose became now not to color all sociopaths as evil or to demonize them, but to shed moderate on a disease that is often misunderstood and to empower the ones who've been victimized with the useful aid of sociopaths.

As we drift earlier, I want to depart you with some key takeaways that I desire will guide you on your journey in the direction of recuperation and reclaiming your lifestyles.

First and fundamental, don't forget that you aren't accountable for the moves and behavior of a sociopath. Their conduct is a mirrored picture of their very non-public sickness and has not some thing to do with you. Do not blame your self or internalize their hurtful words and moves.

Secondly, do no longer underestimate the electricity of setting obstacles. This can be a tough project while managing a professional manipulator, however it's miles important to your nicely-being. Know your limits and keep on with them, notwithstanding the reality that it way decreasing ties with the sociopath.

Additionally, remember your gut and be aware of purple flags. Sociopaths are professionals at deception and may be very fascinating, but there are continuously warning signs that assist you to choose out them. If some factor feels off or too fantastic to be actual, take a step lower once more and reevaluate the state of affairs.

It is also crucial to are searching for beneficial resource from cherished ones or specialists. Dealing with a sociopathic relationship can be distinctly maintaining apart and overwhelming, however you do no longer should face it by myself. Reach out to buddies and family who care approximately your well-being, and preserve in thoughts attempting to find treatment to help you gadget and heal from the trauma.

Lastly, I need to inspire you to keep in your adventure in the direction of restoration and increase. It won't be easy, but recognize that you have the strength and resilience inside you to conquer this enjoy and emerge stronger and wiser.

As we look to the future, my want is for more recognition and records of sociopathy further to extra belongings and resource for the ones who have been affected by it. Let us maintain to teach ourselves and unfold reputation, in order that we are able to create a more solid and in addition empathetic worldwide for all.

Throughout this e-book, we've delved into the internal workings of a sociopath and the way they will be capable of manage and control the ones round them. We have referred to the signs and signs and symptoms and symptoms to appearance out for and coping strategies that will help you navigate through a sociopathic dating. We have also explored the reasons why you could have stayed with a sociopath and the steps you can take to interrupt unfastened.

But now, it's time to do so and make a alternate on your life.

Call to Action: Step out of denial and take control of your existence.

The first step in shifting in advance is to widely known the fact of the situation. Stop making excuses for the sociopath's behavior and stop blaming your self. You aren't responsible for their actions and you must be dealt with with apprehend and kindness.

Next, it's miles vital to set obstacles and stick with them. This can be tough at the identical time as managing a sociopath, as they may try to control and push your obstacles. But live organisation and upward thrust up for yourself. It can be beneficial to trying to find guide from friends, family, or a therapist all through this technique.

Educate yourself approximately sociopathy and study more about the sickness. This will not most effective help you apprehend your accomplice's behavior, however it is able to moreover empower you to make informed options approximately your courting.

It's also essential to take care of yourself. Living with a sociopath may be emotionally and mentally draining, so it's far crucial to prioritize yourself-care. Make time for sports activities that carry you joy and surround yourself with excellent affects.

Make the choice to go away in case you are in a poisonous and abusive relationship. You want to be in a wholesome and loving courting. Do now not allow the concern of being on my own or the guilt of leaving hold you yet again.

Lastly, allow skip of any expectancy for the sociopath to change. Sociopathy is a persona sickness and cannot be cured or constant. It's not your technique to alternate them, and it's far critical to accept that.

Vision for the Future: A life of freedom and happiness.

As you maintain to your adventure of restoration and self-discovery, envision a future wherein you are no longer under the manipulate of a sociopathic accomplice. Futures wherein you've got were given damaged loose from the cycle of abuse and feature determined peace and happiness.

You also can moreover discover comfort in know-how which you aren't by myself. There are many others who've been in similar conditions and feature come out stronger and wiser. Use your revel in to assist others who can be going via the equal trouble.

Chapter 10: Types Of Toxic Personalities

Narcissists

Embarking on a wild safari through the unpredictable jungle of poisonous personalities, we stumble upon the eccentric area of narcissists. Picture this: a species identified for its flair for self-centered theatrics, an unquenchable thirst for applause, and a mysterious hypersensitive reaction to empathy. To navigate this carnival of ego, one has to grasp the paintings of decoding the unusual behaviors that outline narcissism.

Narcissists, those charismatic chameleons of the social scene, can initially seem as fascinating as a magician pulling rabbits out of a hat. Yet, under the splendid facade, lurks an insatiable starvation for hobby and a deep-seated belief of their entitlement to the highlight. Unveiling the dispositions of these interest-hungry performers consists of spotting their penchant for self-absorption, an unrelenting craving for validation, and a unethical to cope with others like assisting actors of their existence drama.

A hallmark of narcissistic behavior is their grandiosity, a larger-than-lifestyles self-photo that competition Hollywood pc photos. This inflated experience of self serves as their superhero cape, protective them from the kryptonite of vulnerability and inadequacy. Engaging with narcissists turns into a excessive-stakes tightrope stroll, balancing their need for regular applause while averting the pitfalls in their fragile egos.

Empathy, the unsung hero of wholesome relationships, is highly absent inside the narcissistic repertoire. Picture a symphony lacking its conductor; narcissists conflict to recognize or share the feelings of others, often steamrolling over goals and boundaries in their quest for self-gratification. This absence of empathy gadgets the degree for the manipulative theatrics usually hired thru narcissists, leaving a path of emotional casualties of their wake.

In the theater of narcissistic relationships, manipulation, and manage take middle degree. They hold close the art of gaslighting, a intellectual phantasm designed to make victims query their fact. It's like being in a mental funhouse wherein mirrors distort perceptions, eroding self guarantee, and sowing seeds of false impression and self-doubt. Recognizing these foxy manipulations becomes a survival capacity inside the presence of a narcissistic maestro.

Furthermore, narcissists placed on a crown of entitlement, believing they deserve royal remedy and unquestioning compliance from their subjects. This entitlement fuels exploitative conduct, turning relationships into a one-sided transaction in which others are mere pawns in their grand chess undertaking. Grasping the dynamics of entitlement will become a essential device for erecting barriers and protective oneself from being strong within the assisting role of a narcissist's production.

The effect of narcissistic relationships spills beyond the private stage into the grand arenas of society and the professional global. Picture a administrative center below the dictatorship of a narcissistic leader – a toxic theater wherein collaboration takes a back seat, and personal success turns into the solo act, leaving the ensemble in disarray. Navigating the ones dramatic dynamics is crucial for maintaining a healthy artwork environment and preserving one's expert sanity.

Confronting narcissists calls for a careful dance of assertiveness and self-upkeep. Think of it as fencing with a grasp manipulator; establishing crystal-easy boundaries becomes the sword that parries their tries at emotional conquest. Recognizing and retaining one's very own needs at the same time as maintaining off the pitfalls of manipulation is the choreography of this dance. Seeking beneficial useful resource from friends, own family, or the intellectual stage organization may be instrumental in navigating the labyrinth of worrying situations posed by means of manner of narcissistic relationships.

Deciphering the enigma of narcissistic behavior is the essential thing to unlocking the secrets and techniques of handling toxic personalities. While the magnetic appeal of narcissists may to begin with dazzle, beneath the glitter lies a labyrinth of ego-centric twists and turns. Identifying the inclinations associated with narcissism empowers people to navigate relationships with the readability and resilience had to create a degree that prioritizes proper connections and emotional well-being.

Sociopaths

Venturing into the wild territory of poisonous personalities, we encounter the mysterious and regularly perilous region of sociopaths. Armed with a toolkit that boasts a profound loss of empathy, a knack for manipulation, and a blatant push aside for societal norms, those characters turn navigating their difficult conduct proper right into a survival important.

Sociopaths, at the begin appearance, may deliver off the vibes of a seasoned actor hitting their marks with appeal and air of mystery. This preliminary appeal, but, is more like a smokescreen for their real nature. Underneath the appeal lies a stark absence of empathy – a one in all a kind trait that devices sociopaths apart from the regular crowd. Grasping the subtleties of this empathy void is pivotal for recognizing the patterns that outline sociopathy.

The hallmark of sociopathy lies in their handy mastery of manipulation. Armed with an encyclopedic expertise of human emotions and vulnerabilities, sociopaths orchestrate situations tailored to serve their egocentric interests. From subtle emotional nudges to more blatant maneuvers, their bag of tips is continuously targeted on challenge their dreams, oblivious to the collateral harm left of their wake.

Sociopaths proudly show off a lack of regret or guilt for his or her moves. This absence of ethical shackles permits them to have interaction in behaviors that could deliver the relaxation parents on a guilt journey. It's like having a superhero power, allowing them to navigate a moral panorama with out being careworn with the useful aid of the moral problems that manual the majority.

Furthermore, sociopaths are maestros at adopting personas to in shape their targets. Picture them as social chameleons – fascinating and amiable one second, seamlessly morphing proper into a greater competitive or manipulative demeanor because of the fact the script demands. This chameleon-like ability to form-shift their personality adds to the task of identifying sociopaths, as they outcomes mixture into numerous social situations.

In relationships with sociopaths, a acquainted pattern of exploitation emerges. Others grow to be mere equipment for their gain, without any proper emotional connection. This exploitative attitude might occur in monetary trickery, emotional rollercoasters, or maybe more immoderate sorts of damage. Recognizing the signs and symptoms and signs and symptoms of exploitation becomes paramount for extricating oneself from the clutches of a sociopathic relationship.

The impact of sociopathic humans extends past non-public relationships, infiltrating the expert and societal nation-states. Picture a place of job beneath the sway of a sociopathic colleague or boss – manipulation taking walks rampant, teamwork crumbling, and a poisonous fog settling over the place of job. Recognizing and navigating those dynamics will become the oxygen mask for maintaining a wholesome art work environment and safeguarding one's expert nicely-being.

Sociopaths regularly show off impulsive behaviors and a lack of long-term planning, which encompass a typhoon tearing via relationships and leaving chaos of their wake.

It's like dealing with a stress of nature – a whirlwind that would upend the whole thing in its route. Understanding the man or woman of sociopathic impulsivity becomes vital for predicting and handling the functionality debris scattered across numerous elements of lifestyles.

Spotting sociopathic behavior needs a Sherlock Holmes degree of deduction. They may also exhibit superficial enchantment, an inflated sense of self esteem, and an insatiable need for stimulation, constantly chasing new thrills without a care for the rollercoaster's impact on others. This attraction frequently conceals a shadowy reality, annoying a eager eye for the subtleties that betray the right nature of a sociopathic individual.

The absence of a moral compass in sociopaths allows them to engage in deceit with the finesse of a con artist. They can spin lies outcomes, weaving an internet of deception that serves their goals. This deceit is sort of a masterfully crafted illusion, tough to unveil as sociopaths adeptly preserve a façade of honesty while concealing their actual motives.

Confronting sociopaths necessitates a combination of vigilance, assertiveness, and self-protection. Picture it as a excessive-stakes poker sport; putting in clean obstacles becomes the royal flush that mitigates the capacity harm of their manipulative approaches. Recognizing the symptoms and signs and symptoms of manipulation and exploitation empowers individuals to go out the stage left from toxic relationships, protective their emotional properly-being like a pro Hollywood huge call.

Grasping the intricacies of sociopathic behavior is like wielding a compass thru the complicated panorama of poisonous personalities. Sociopaths, with their attraction and manipulation, present a totally particular set of demanding situations that demand an alertness to their tendencies and behaviors. Identifying and facts the nature of sociopathy empowers individuals to defend themselves from the ability storm those human beings can unleash and cultivate an environment that prioritizes proper connections and emotional nicely-being.

Psychopaths

Embarking on a rollercoaster ride through the maze of poisonous personalities, we delve into the complex and regularly menacing realm of psychopaths. These characters wield a completely precise arsenal marked by means of manner of a profound lack of empathy, a mastery of manipulation, and a penchant for delinquent behavior. Navigating the twists and turns of psychopathic behavior will become a survival skills, guarding in competition to the capability havoc they could wreak.

At first appearance, psychopaths may as properly be famous man or woman actors charming an intention market with enchantment and air of thriller. This preliminary attraction acts as a smoke show

show, concealing their true nature. Beneath the attraction lies a stark absence of empathy — a center trait setting psychopaths aside from the relaxation. Grasping the subtleties of this empathy void is fundamental to figuring out the behavioral patterns that define psychopathy.

A defining feature of psychopathy is the smart finesse with which they manage others. Psychopaths own a keen information of human feelings and vulnerabilities, using this information to choreograph eventualities that serve their self-hobby. From subtle emotional maneuvers to greater blatant tactics, their bag of suggestions is continuously geared towards accomplishing their goals with out a 2d notion for the collateral harm.

Psychopaths exhibit a lack of remorse or guilt, granting them a intellectual benefit in assignment behaviors that might supply others on a guilt adventure. It's like having a superhero power, allowing them to navigate a moral landscape without the moral constraints that guide the majority.

Moreover, psychopaths display top notch adaptability, seamlessly adopting personas aligned with their instant goals. Picture them as social chameleons – tremendous and captivating one second, effortlessly transitioning to a greater aggressive or manipulative demeanor as instances dictate. This capability to alternate personalities presents to the challenge of identifying psychopaths, as they consequences mixture into numerous social situations.

In relationships with psychopaths, a habitual challenge depend involves manipulation and exploitation. Others emerge as mere pawns of their interest, lacking any real emotional connection. This exploitative mind-set may additionally moreover take region in economic deceit, emotional abuse, or extra immoderate types of harm. Identifying the signs and symptoms and signs and symptoms of exploitation will become paramount for escaping the clutches of a psychopathic courting.

The effect of psychopathic people extends past personal relationships, infiltrating professional and societal spheres. In the administrative center, a psychopathic colleague or supervisor also can interact in manipulation, growing a poisonous environment characterised with the beneficial resource of deceit, loss of empathy, and an undermining of teamwork. Navigating those dynamics is important for keeping a healthful paintings environment and safeguarding one's expert well-being.

Psychopaths often display impulsive behaviors and a lack of prolonged-time period planning, contributing to a path of chaos of their wake. Their impulsivity, coupled with a brush aside for results, effects in a terrible force just like a hurricane tearing thru relationships. Understanding the man or woman of psychopathic impulsivity turns into vital for predicting and dealing with the ability fallout within the direction of severa factors of life.

Detecting psychopathic behavior requires honing one's capability to understand the red flags and warning signs and symptoms and signs and symptoms. Psychopaths might also exhibit superficial appeal, a grandiose experience of self esteem, and a need for stimulation, continuously searching for new thrills with out a deal with the impact on others. This outdoor enchantment often conceals a darker reality, annoying a eager eye for the subtleties that betray the right nature of a psychopathic man or woman.

The absence of a ethical compass in psychopaths lets in them to interact in deceit without compunction. They lie effects, spinning an internet of deception that serves their dreams. This deceit may be difficult to find, as psychopaths skillfully hold a façade of honesty at the equal time as concealing their right reasons.

Dealing with psychopaths requires a combination of vigilance, assertiveness, and self-protection. Establishing clean obstacles will become essential for mitigating the capacity harm in their manipulative techniques. Recognizing the symptoms of manipulation and exploitation empowers individuals to exit the diploma of toxic relationships and guard their emotional properly-being.

Comprehending the intricacies of psychopathic conduct is like the use of the waves of a stormy sea in the complicated landscape of poisonous personalities. Psychopaths, with their attraction and manipulation, gift a completely unique set of demanding situations that name for heightened consciousness in their traits and behaviors. Identifying and expertise the character of psychopathy empowers people to guard themselves from the capability storm the ones human beings can unleash and fosters an environment that prioritizes proper connections and emotional properly-being.

Chapter 11: Early Warning Signs

Behavioral Patterns

As we venture into the arena of interpreting the complexities of toxic relationships, a essential checkpoint emerges – information the preliminary caution signs and symptoms and signs. These cues, much like ambitious strokes on a canvas, display a good deal approximately the character of poisonous impacts. They offer insights that empower individuals to navigate the tricky panorama in their social circles with heightened interest and wit.

One apparent behavioral pattern signaling ability toxicity is a everyday loss of empathy. Toxic people frequently show off an loss of capability or reluctance to apprehend and percentage the emotions of others. This translates into dismissive attitudes in the direction of the emotions and desires of those around them. Spotting this early sign is pivotal, forming the foundation for information the functionality effect of such individuals on one's emotional well-being.

Another noteworthy behavioral sample involves manipulative dispositions. Whether narcissists, sociopaths, or psychopaths, toxic human beings grasp the art work of subtle or overt manipulation to achieve their goals. From emotional play on vulnerabilities to strategic gaslighting, distorting fact to sow seeds of doubt – figuring out the ones manipulative tactics early on is important. It serves as a defend, stopping the erosion of one's sense of self.

A red flag often waved in toxic relationships is a pattern of steady complaint and belittlement. Toxic people lease various processes to undermine the vanity and self guarantee of those spherical them. Derogatory comments, normal nitpicking, or insidious emotional abuse may be a part of this arsenal. Recognizing this behavioral pattern allows humans to defend themselves from the corrosive outcomes of non-stop negativity.

Isolation is some one of a kind brilliant behavioral pattern signaling toxicity in relationships. Toxic humans subtly or overtly manipulate their objectives to distance themselves from friends, family, or help networks. This isolation complements the poisonous character's manipulate, making it tough for the victim to seeking out out of doors perspectives. Recognizing the early signs and symptoms of isolation lets in people to proactively hold their social connections and resist the grip of poisonous effect.

Inconsistency in behavior is an indicator of toxic humans. They may also moreover present a fascinating facade one 2nd and unexpectedly transition to hostility or indifference the following. This unpredictable behavior creates instability and unease in relationships. Identifying this erratic sample early on lets in people to navigate relationships with heightened warning, minimizing functionality emotional turbulence as a result of the poisonous person's transferring demeanor.

Toxicity frequently manifests in a pattern of boundary violations. Toxic human beings brush aside private boundaries and autonomy, intruding into emotional, bodily, or intellectual area. Recognizing the ones early signs and symptoms of boundary-crossing is vital for putting in and reinforcing non-public limits, stopping the gradual erosion of one's autonomy and self-appreciate.

Moreover, a steady sample of deflection and blame-transferring is a pink flag in toxic relationships. When confronted with their conduct, poisonous human beings might also additionally deflect duty and shift blame onto others. This evasion tactic shields their fragile self-picture and deflects scrutiny. Recognizing this pattern permits people to navigate conflicts with readability and avoid being ensnared in a cycle of blame and manipulation.

Understanding the early caution signs of poisonous relationships is just like interpreting bold strokes on a canvas. Recognizing the behavioral styles associated with toxicity empowers human beings to navigate their social landscapes with discernment and resilience. By identifying purple flags which consist of lack of empathy, manipulative dispositions, ordinary complaint, isolation, inconsistency, boundary violations, and blame-moving, people can proactively defend their emotional nicely-being and installation a foundation for healthful, reciprocal relationships.

Manipulative Tactics

Embarking at the escapade of deciphering the enigmatic international of poisonous relationships, a crucial quest lies in spotting the early caution symptoms, mainly the labyrinth of manipulative techniques. These strategic maneuvers, reminiscent of a cunning chess player's calculated moves, regularly wave pink flags, handing over vital insights into the essence of poisonous affects. Grasping those manipulative strategies is vital for humans to meander via the intricacies of their social circles with wit and resilience.

One frequently encountered manipulative tactic consists of the artful dance of gaslighting. Toxic humans, whether narcissists, sociopaths, or psychopaths, are maestros at distorting fact to sow seeds of doubt in their sufferers' minds. Gaslighting, like a pervasive fog, chips away on the sufferer's confidence, fostering a experience of false impression and self-doubt. Discerning the nuances of gaslighting early on is paramount for maintaining highbrow clarity and safeguarding emotional well-being.

Another strategic manipulation often employed is the theatrical play of emotional strings. Toxic humans, armed with the expertise of human feelings and vulnerabilities, diploma situations to serve their self-interest. This may also additionally need to consist of guilt-tripping, gambling at the victim's sympathies, or orchestrating emotional turmoil to benefit manage. Spotting those emotional manipulation strategies early on empowers humans to erect resilient barriers, thwarting the toxic individual's calculated ploys.

A recurrent difficulty in manipulative strategies is using enchantment and air of thriller as a amazing veil. Toxic human beings frequently don a facade of friendliness and likability, drawing unsuspecting souls into their orbit. This initial attraction acts as a disarming maneuver, making targets more vulnerable to manipulation. Recognizing the chasm amongst floor charm and underlying reasons is critical for individuals to navigate relationships with smart discernment.

Manipulative maestros might also furthermore lodge to weaving a fake narrative or assuming the victim's function to elicit sympathy and assist. This cunning tactic includes distorting statistics, exaggerating conditions, or framing themselves as unjustly persecuted. Recognizing the manipulation inherent within the ones fabricated narratives permits humans to significantly take a look at furnished records and forestall manipulation into assisting the poisonous individual's schedule.

The tactical use of triangulation is another strategic manipulation that often surfaces in poisonous relationships. This includes cunningly manipulating communication and relationships amongst specific events to instigate conflicts and installation manage. Toxic people can also sow discord thru spreading wrong statistics, instigating misunderstandings, or pitting people closer to every other. Detecting those manipulative maneuvers early on empowers humans to keep open and sincere verbal exchange, resisting entanglement inside the net of triangulation.

Furthermore, toxic tacticians may also additionally installation the manipulation tactic of intermittent reinforcement to hold manages over their objectives. This consists of alternating amongst rewards and punishments to preserve human beings unsure and counting on the poisonous man or woman's approval. The sporadic nature of fine and terrible reinforcement creates a intellectual loop that may be tough to interrupt. Recognizing this manipulative cycle early on is vital for humans to claim their autonomy and withstand being ensnared in a cycle of control.

Covert aggression is each extraordinary subtle manipulation tactic that toxic human beings may additionally wield. This includes subtly undermining others through passive-aggressive behaviors, backhanded compliments, or veiled insults. Recognizing the symptoms of covert aggression equips human beings with a heightened reputation of the subtle tries to chip away at their self belief and shallowness.

Navigating the complicated chessboard of manipulative strategies in toxic relationships desires acute interest of the subtle movements employed through toxic human beings. From the dance of gaslighting and emotional manipulation to the strategic use of appeal, faux narratives, triangulation, intermittent reinforcement, and covert aggression, deciphering those techniques empowers individuals to preserve clarity, erect sturdy barriers, and withstand manipulation. Recognizing the early warning signs of manipulative behaviors lays the foundation for navigating social landscapes with keen discernment, safeguarding emotional nicely-being, and nurturing healthy, reciprocal relationships.

Chapter 12: Assessing Your Social Circle

Friendships

In the colorful mosaic of our lives, friendships add a touch of shade, influencing our reviews, views, and emotional properly-being. Evaluating your social circle consists of diving into the complex dynamics of friendships, comprehending their effect, and smartly deciding on to assemble a community that fosters your growth and happiness.

Friendships, similar to a palette of severa strokes on a canvas, are available numerous colorings and intensities. Some friendships are like energetic watercolors, bringing pride and spontaneity. These are the buddies with whom you percentage laughs, adventures, and a revel in of camaraderie. Evaluating the superb elements of these friendships method recognizing mutual help, shared pursuits, and real connections that make contributions to a active and beautiful social circle.

Yet, not all strokes on the canvas radiate positivity. Some friendships may also lean within the route of darker solar solar shades, introducing complexities and demanding conditions. These might be relationships marked via manner of competition, jealousy, or an choppy offer-and-take. Assessing such friendships calls for a keen eye to choose out out horrible patterns and determine whether or not retaining the relationship offers enrichment or becomes a draining enterprise.

While navigating the terrain of friendships, prioritizing the reliability and trustworthiness of your social circle turns into paramount. Trust acts because the adhesive shielding friendships together, fostering openness and vulnerability. Trustworthy buddies stand strong during tough instances and cheer for your victories. Assessing the trustworthiness of friendships involves reflecting on the consistency of aid, the capacity to speak in self belief to every one of a kind, and the shared revel in of reliability forming the inspiration of believe.

Friendships are extra than floor-degree interactions; they dive into the sector of emotional intelligence. Gauging emotional intelligence inside your social circle manner spotting pals' ability to empathize, recognize, and navigate emotional nuances. Emotionally sensible buddies deepen connections, providing meaningful insights and manual in some unspecified time in the future of emotional turbulence. Evaluating emotional intelligence in friendships contributes to a nurturing and sturdy social material.

In the location of friendships, reciprocity acts as a vital strand, threading thru the offer-and-take dynamics that symbolize healthful connections. Assessing reciprocity on your social circle involves reflecting on whether or not there's a stability inside the change of guide, time, and power. Reciprocal friendships are marked with the useful resource of the usage of mutual efforts to keep the connection, make contributions actually to each unique's lives, and have a superb time shared joys. Recognizing reciprocity styles publications alternatives on which friendships to cultivate.

Much like the body of a canvas, boundaries delineate the contours of friendships, defining the space wherein humans engage and percentage critiques. Evaluating the strength of barriers for your social circle involves reflecting on whether or not there's a wholesome stability among closeness and individual autonomy. Respect for barriers guarantees that friendships stay enriching with out turning into suffocating. Assessing boundary power permits for changes contributing to the sturdiness and nicely-being of friendships.

Diversity inside your social circle enriches reminiscences and views. Evaluating the variety of friendships includes reflecting on the style of backgrounds, interests, and worldviews represented. Diverse friendships enlarge horizons, assignment assumptions, and decorate the material of existence.

Recognizing the rate of variety fosters an inclusive and dynamic social surroundings.

In the dynamic realm of friendships, war is an inevitable a part of the choreography. Assessing struggle selection internal your social circle consists of reflecting on how variations are addressed, resolved, or navigated. Healthy friendships view conflicts as boom opportunities, fostering open verbal exchange and mutual information. Evaluating struggle selection dynamics contributes to the resilience and durability of connections.

Friendships aren't static; they evolve and redesign over the years. Assessing the increase and evolution of friendships consists of reflecting on whether or not or now not the ones connections align with non-public development. Healthy friendships useful resource character boom, encourage aspirations, and adapt to converting life dynamics. Evaluating increase interior friendships publications choices on which connections to nurture.

In the expansive canvas of friendships, poisonous relationships stand as dark splotches, threatening the concord of the overall composition. Evaluating poisonous elements consists of spotting crimson flags like manipulation, deceit, or steady negativity. Toxic friendships can erode well-being, and comparing their presence permits for conscious selections to distance oneself from adverse affects. Addressing toxicity inner friendships contributes to the appearance of a supportive and uplifting social fabric.

Assessing your social circle, with a focal point on friendships, is a savvy exploration of the various threads contributing to the hard mosaic of your lifestyles. Friendships, with their numerous colours and textures, appreciably impact well-being and testimonies. By reflecting on elements like receive as real with, emotional intelligence, reciprocity, boundaries, variety, conflict choice, increase, and toxicity, you empower yourself to navigate the dynamic dance of friendships with knowledge and intentionality, making sure the threads woven into your mosaic make a contribution to a colorful and pleasing life.

Romantic Relationships

Embarking on a profound day trip via the landscape of our social interactions, romantic relationships floor as a pivotal layer, injecting intricacy and depth into our interwoven lives. Delving into the nuances of your social circle consists of taking a higher check the brilliant dynamics of romantic connections, unveiling the complexities that mold our emotional reviews and effect our properly-being.

In the widespread spectrum of romantic relationships, from the preliminary sparks of infatuation to the mature depths of prolonged-time period strength of will, acknowledging this variety requires an beauty of the diverse array of romantic studies and the infinite connections that would blossom. It's an admission that each romantic dating possesses its unique tendencies, defying the limitations of a standardized mould.

As the curtains rise at the early stages of romantic entanglement, chemistry gracefully takes center diploma. Assessing romantic functionality needs an data of this chemistry – the magnetic enchantment shared laughter, and the intoxicating thrill of coming across someone new. Yet, relying totally on chemistry proves inadequate; compatibility steps onto the extent as a critical player. Unraveling compatibility consists of an exploration of shared values, existence goals, and the ability for a harmonious future.

Trust stands due to the fact the bedrock of putting up with romantic connections. Scrutinizing the trustworthiness of a romantic partner consists of contemplation on the consistency of movements, honesty, and reliability. Trust acts due to the fact the catalyst for vulnerability and openness, cultivating an environment wherein every humans sense consistent in revealing their actual selves. The assessment of agree with within a romantic dating contributes to the development of a resilient foundation.

Communication, much like the lifeblood coursing via the veins of romantic relationships, plays a important function. The assessment of conversation dynamics encompasses the popularity of the capability to explicit emotions, interact in sizeable conversations, and navigate disagreements constructively. Effective communique nurtures emotional intimacy and understanding, directing the trajectory of constructing a connection that endures the trials of time.

The nuanced dance amongst togetherness and independence paints the canvas of a healthy romantic relationship. Gauging the equilibrium of character autonomy involves contemplation on whether or not both partners hold a experience of self amidst shared studies. Valuing non-public place and pastimes fosters a connection wherein human beings can evolve collectively with out surrendering their identities. The assessment of this equilibrium contributes to the cultivation of a relationship flourishing on mutual guide and independence.

While physical intimacy is sincerely a aspect, the profound intensity of emotional connection defines a meaningful romantic relationship. Scrutinizing emotional intimacy calls for a deep dive into the capability to percentage fears, dreams, and vulnerabilities. This emotional connection transcends superficial interactions, weaving a bond that withstands demanding conditions and exults in triumphs. The evaluation of the emotional depth of a romantic courting contributes to a experience of contentment and protection.

Challenges, the inevitable companions of any romantic journey, necessitate evaluation. Contemplating a romantic dating includes pondered photograph on how conflicts are addressed and resolved. Healthy relationships apprehend traumatic situations as possibilities for boom, with the capacity to navigate disagreements constructively, look at from conflicts, and emerge stronger defining the resilience of a romantic bond. The assessment of war choice dynamics contributes to the sturdiness and profundity of the connection.

Passion, an ever-evolving stress, stays a pivotal detail in enduring romantic connections. Evaluating ardour includes spotting the long-lasting pleasure, choice, and emotional fervor. Sustaining ardour wishes continuous attempt, creativity, and a commitment to keeping the flame alive. The evaluation of ardour's presence contributes to a romantic dating that remains colourful and pleasurable through the various stages of life.

Scrutinizing a romantic relationship encompasses contemplation of lifestyles goals and destiny alignment. It's an exploration of whether or not or now not each companions envision a nicely matched destiny, sharing comparable aspirations and values. Evaluating destiny alignment courses options at the ability durability of the relationship, ensuring that each humans are progressing in tandem towards shared dreams.

In the complicated mosaic of romantic relationships, poisonous elements can solid a shadow over the general composition. Assessing functionality toxicity includes recognizing crimson flags like manipulation, manage, or persistent negativity. Toxic romantic relationships have the capability to corrode well-being, and comparing their presence allows for aware options to distance oneself from bad affects. Confronting toxicity within a romantic relationship contributes to the mounted order of a supportive and uplifting connection.

Romantic relationships are dynamic, present system a herbal evolution. Assessing the increase and evolution of a romantic connection involves contemplation on whether or not the relationship aligns with non-public improvement. Healthy relationships manual character growth, adapting to converting dynamics and disturbing situations. The assessment of increase within a romantic relationship publications choices on which connections to nurture and domesticate.

The scrutiny of your social circle, with a focal point on romantic relationships, consists of a nuanced exploration of the layers contributing to the complicated cloth of your lifestyles. Romantic connections, with their numerous research and profound influences, considerably impact your emotional properly-being. By reflecting on factors like chemistry, compatibility, don't forget, communication, autonomy, emotional intimacy, conflict choice, ardour, future alignment, caution signs and signs and signs, and evolution, you empower your self to navigate the complexities of romantic relationships with statistics and intentionality, making sure that the threads woven into this hard mosaic make a contribution to a colourful and satisfying life.

Workplace Dynamics

The place of work isn't simplest a space for expert responsibilities; it's a microcosm of social interactions that drastically effect our every day lives. Assessing one's social circle involves delving into the intricacies of place of business relationships, and statistics the nuances that shape expert connections and have an effect on our regular well-being.

In the expert realm, relationships form a completely specific tapestry – colleagues, supervisors, subordinates, and mentors make contributions to this elaborate format. These relationships are not absolutely transactional; they devise emotional weight and play a pivotal role in shaping the art work environment. Assessing the expert tapestry entails information the dynamics of diverse relationships inside the place of business and recognizing their have an effect on on character growth and career trajectory.

Workplaces often entail hierarchies and power structures that have an effect on the dynamics of interactions. Navigating those hierarchies calls for a keen interest of strength dynamics, statistics how electricity is wielded, and the way humans navigate interior the ones systems. Recognition of the subtle nuances in energy dynamics permits people to navigate expert relationships with international relations and foresight.

Professional achievement is intricately associated with the energy of professional networks. Assessing place of job dynamics consists of actively constructing and nurturing powerful expert networks. This consists of figuring out key influencers, fostering relationships with colleagues throughout departments, and tasty in collaborative efforts. A sturdy expert community contributes no longer simplest to career improvement however moreover to a supportive and enriching paintings surroundings.

Effective communique is the backbone of successful place of business dynamics. Assessing the intricacies of place of business relationships calls for an expertise of severa conversation styles. Individuals inside a workplace frequently convey distinct communication picks and strategies. Recognizing the ones patterns, whether or not or no longer or now not they may be direct or oblique, assertive or diplomatic, is essential for fostering smooth and effective communique. A nuanced comprehension of communication styles lets in individuals to navigate administrative center conversations with finesse.

In the complicated net of place of business dynamics, conflicts are inevitable. Assessing one's social circle in a expert context includes an exploration of war selection strategies. Healthy places of work embody conflicts as possibilities for boom and innovation. Understanding how conflicts are addressed, whether or not thru open speak, mediation, or exclusive mechanisms, is vital for preserving a fantastic art work surroundings. The functionality to navigate conflicts constructively contributes to resilient administrative center relationships.

Mentorship is a effective strain in place of work dynamics, gambling a pivotal function in expert development. Assessing the impact of mentorship consists of recognizing the rate of professional colleagues guiding and assisting profession growth. Establishing mentor-mentee relationships can significantly affect one's trajectory inside an organisation. Understanding the way to are searching for, set up, and contribute to mentorship dynamics is vital to navigating the expert landscape.

Workplace dynamics are regularly entangled with politics – a diffused dance of impact, alliances, and strategic moves. Assessing one's social circle within the place of business consists of a discerning hobby of those political undercurrents. Recognizing energy performs, unspoken alliances, and the effect of organizational lifestyle on choice-making is essential for successfully navigating workplace politics. A clever statistics of those dynamics permits individuals to make knowledgeable options and strategically function themselves in the corporation.

The not unusual environment internal a place of business notably influences character properly-being and expert satisfaction. Assessing administrative center dynamics includes cultivating a amazing paintings environment. This consists of fostering a way of existence of collaboration, recognizing and appreciating colleagues' contributions, and actively taking part in duties that make contributions to a healthful place of business lifestyle. A excellent paintings surroundings now not excellent complements venture satisfaction however additionally fosters strong expert connections.

Navigating workplace dynamics calls for a sensitive stability among professionalism and authenticity. Assessing one's social circle at art work includes expertise at the same time as to stick to expert norms and while to convey one's authentic self to the main facet. Striking this balance contributes to real connections, preserve in thoughts, and a chunk environment in which people experience visible and valued. The capability to authentically have interaction with colleagues fosters sizeable place of work relationships.

In the evolving landscape of labor, far flung and digital dynamics have become increasingly regular. Assessing workplace dynamics now extends to the digital realm, in which verbal exchange happens via video display units and virtual systems. Understanding the nuances of virtual communication, building connections in a much flung placing, and leveraging era for effective collaboration are vital components of navigating contemporary-day workplace dynamics.

Diversity and inclusion are essential additives of contemporary workplace dynamics. Assessing one's social circle at paintings consists of recognizing and embracing range throughout severa dimensions, together with but not constrained to ethnicity, gender, and records. Creating an inclusive paintings surroundings promotes collaboration, innovation, and a experience of belonging. Understanding the significance of range and actively contributing to an inclusive workplace culture is crucial for fostering fantastic place of business dynamics.

Chapter 13: Emotional And Psychological Impact

Recognizing the Toll on Your Well-being

Embarking on a journey to get to the bottom of the depths of emotional and intellectual effect is like setting sail within the vast sea of human recollections. We navigate the fascinating complexities that mildew the contours of one's properly-being, requiring savvy facts of the myriad elements shaping emotional and mental states within the human odyssey.

In this kaleidoscope of feelings and intellectual nuances, a spectrum unfolds, painting the canvas of our internal global with numerous colorations. From the peaks of pleasure to the valleys of strain, an individual's emotional properly-being will become a mirror reflecting lifestyles' myriad critiques. It transcends fleeting emotions, embracing the overall first rate of emotional life, fostering adaptability, and sculpting a pleasing outlook on the grand mural of lifestyles.

Within this emotional landscape, the dance among mental resilience and adversity takes middle degree. Life, adorned with triumphs and tribulations, is a tale wherein assessing intellectual resilience consists of interpreting the factors forging intellectual power. Coping mechanisms, resource structures, and a growth-oriented mind-set grow to be the brushstrokes building mental resilience, allowing people to get better from the dramatic plot twists scripted within the novel of existence.

Stress, a ubiquitous stress inside the riveting tale of contemporary life, emerges as a big influencer of emotional equilibrium. Chronic pressure, even as it becomes a steadfast accomplice, can tilt emotional stability and compromise mental resilience. Recognizing the signs and signs and symptoms of strain beckons introspection and an attention of its precise manifestations in every character, inciting intentional efforts to play the hero and mitigate its impact.

At the depths of the emotional panorama lie anxiety and despair, profound valleys that would stable a widespread shadow on properly-being. Recognizing the ones intellectual health stressful conditions includes breaking the stigma surrounding them, and growing an surroundings wherein people enjoy snug looking for aid. Assessing the toll of anxiety and depression goals a complete information of their manifestations and the importance of well timed intervention, playing the feature of a realistic sage, and searching for professional help.

Positive psychology provides a glowing twist to the story through focusing on strengths, virtues, and factors contributing to a satisfying life. Amidst the emotional landscape, cultivating gratitude, schooling mindfulness, and fostering tremendous connections grow to be pivotal plot elements. Assessing the impact of terrific psychology on emotional and mental states encourages humans to be lively protagonists, accomplishing sports that sell joy and fulfillment.

Relationships, the ones pivotal characters inside the complicated dance of human connections, turn out to be key gamers in the narrative. Recognizing the toll on properly-being propels an exploration into the notable of relationships, from familial bonds to friendships and romantic entanglements. Assessing the impact of relationships involves deciphering the jobs of empathy, effective conversation, and mutual assist, ensuring a sturdy emotional manual device.

Trauma, a haunting subplot echoing through emotional and mental nicely-being, leaves imprints traumatic sensitive acknowledgment and recuperation. Recognizing the toll on properly-being necessitates a compassionate technique, integrating healing interventions and resilience-building techniques to navigate the course towards healing. The grand tapestry of nicely-being extends past feelings and psychology, intertwining with the dance of bodily health.

Recognizing the toll on nicely-being consists of an acknowledgment of the mind-body connection, where bodily health weaves its threads into the emotional tapestry. Assessing the impact of physical health on emotional properly-being encourages holistic self-care practices, encompassing exercising, vitamins, and appropriate enough relaxation to boost average nicely-being.

The societal narrative weaves norms, expectancies, and cultural impacts that form our perceptions of highbrow health. Recognizing the toll on properly-being requires an exam of societal attitudes closer to intellectual fitness, aiming to destigmatize conversations, advocating for inclusive and available highbrow health resources, and rewriting the societal script. Assessing the impact of cultural affects includes embracing variety in highbrow fitness reviews and fostering a supportive surroundings for all characters.

Personal success emerges as a radiant subplot inside the well-being novel, beckoning an introspective adventure into private values, passions, and aspirations. Recognizing the toll on well-being consists of aligning life with motive, and nurturing a enjoy of which means that that contributes to common properly-being. The digital age, with its incessant skip of data and connectivity, poses stressful conditions that want delicate navigation.

Recognizing the toll on nicely-being includes a conscious voyage thru the digital landscape, putting obstacles, and fostering a healthy relationship with era. Assessing the impact of virtual behavior on emotional and mental states encourages humans to be savvy protagonists, setting a balance that promotes properly-being in an increasingly more interconnected worldwide.

The exploration of emotional and highbrow impact well-knownshows a canvas adorned with tough dimensions that extensively have an effect on properly-being. Recognizing the toll for your nicely-being wishes a holistic statistics of emotions, psychological states, resilience, strain, intellectual fitness demanding situations, excessive nice psychology, relationships, trauma, physical fitness, cultural influences, private fulfillment, digital conduct, and the continued adventure of self-discovery. By navigating the ones dimensions with attention and intentionality, people empower themselves to craft a resilient and exciting masterpiece of emotional and mental nicely-being.

Chapter 14: Establishing Boundaries

Setting Healthy Limits

In lifestyles's adventurous escapade, the knack for placing boundaries becomes a survival capability, similar to crafting a personal blueprint for properly-being. It's no longer quite plenty claiming your physical territory but a savvy maneuver thru the mazes of human interplay, self-safety, and constructing connections that certainly increase your journey.

To maintain near the essence of limitations is to honor your dignity and famend your non-public desires. At its middle, it's approximately drawing invisible traces that declare wherein you end and others start. This know-how activates a journey into your values, consolation zones, and the realization that, yes, it's no longer simply best but downright critical to position your properly-being at the forefront.

Boundaries are to be had a spectrum, starting from the tangible fort of private vicinity to the intangible geographical regions of emotional and highbrow limits. On the concrete facet, setting physical limitations manner proclaiming your alternatives approximately personal area, touch, and the coveted realm of privateness. Venturing further into the spectrum, emotional barriers dictate the amount to that you're snug sharing your innermost feelings and reviews, underscoring the want to keep emotional independence.

Crafting a blueprint for correctly-being requires a virtuoso within the paintings of announcing no – a cornerstone in boundary architecture. It's a statement that a while and strength are valuable commodities with limits. This involves a discerning evaluation of your priorities and a profound knowledge that committing to every project can also moreover lead you right away to burnout. Saying no isn't a refusal; it's a way to preserve your potential for high-quality contributions and keep a harmonious equilibrium for your life.

Preserving emotional power emerges as every other critical act in boundary choreography. Emotional barriers are the unsung heroes safeguarding your highbrow nicely-being, guiding you on on the identical time as to dive into conversations, figuring out your emotional funding in relationships, and performing as shields towards emotional exhaustion. This skills permits you to live actual to yourself amidst the complex ballet of human connections.

In the vicinity of relationships, boundary-placing isn't approximately building fortresses; it's about placing a sensitive balance among independence and connection. Relationship obstacles entail placing expectations, articulating desires, and respecting the autonomy of every parties involved. By spelling out limitations actually, you pave the manner for relationships that are not most effective collectively supportive but additionally respectful of each one-of-a-kind's forte.

The professional place unfurls a separate canvas for boundary craftsmanship. Workplace barriers involve capping workloads, defining expectations with colleagues, and acknowledging the sacred significance of maintaining a work-existence balance. Erecting crystal-smooth professional limitations contributes to a career trajectory that's no longer just a achievement but moreover sustainable and pleasant.

Understanding the fluidity of boundaries is vital, in particular within the realm of relationships. Recognizing warning signs and symptoms urges people to assess whether or not their set barriers are despite the fact that serving their top notch pursuits. Adjusting boundaries in relationships needs open communique, moments of self-reflected photo, and a willingness to bop with the evolving dynamics of private and expert connections.

Cultivating self-focus is the bedrock of being an adept boundary sculptor. It requires delving into the deep recesses of private triggers, and luxury zones, and the capacity to articulate those insights to others. Self-focus empowers you to set limitations that resonate on the aspect of your values and add clearly for your conventional properly-being.

One of the hurdles in boundary-placing is overcoming guilt, regularly fueled with the aid of way of societal expectations or a choice to be a crowd-pleaser. Defeating guilt consists of spotting that obstacles aren't a rejection of others; they're a form of self-care, a approach to prioritize non-public nicely-being with out succumbing to the snares of external pressures.

Establishing boundaries is a collaborative affair, especially in relationships. Cultivating a way of life of admire necessitates mutual expertise and negotiations on obstacles. This includes open verbal exchange, lively listening, and a pledge to foster an surroundings wherein every people experience stated, valued, and deeply understood.

As people navigate existence's labyrinth, resilience in the face of boundary demanding situations turns into an art work shape. Challenges also can sprout from out of doors pressures, societal norms, or the chameleon-like nature of relationships. Resilience includes adapting boundaries as wished, studying from tales, and status employer to your commitment to non-public nicely-being.

The craft of adaptive barriers lies in maintaining a stability among flexibility and firmness. Flexibility permits adjustments primarily based totally on evolving situations, at the same time as firmness guarantees your middle values and well-being stay untarnished. It's a diffused dance that humans draw near through self-reputation, self-compassion, and an knowledge that barriers are a dynamic component of personal boom.

As humans maintain close to the critical position of barriers, offering boundary talents becomes a present for the following generation. This entails modeling wholesome boundary-placing behaviors, offering smart advocate on navigating numerous contexts, and instilling the expertise that putting barriers isn't a protective circulate but an empowering act contributing to typical nicely-being.

In essence, organising obstacles isn't always anyone-time gig; it's a perpetual adventure of self-care. It's a dynamic tool that needs self-awareness, adaptability, and a willpower to drafting a non-public blueprint for effectively-being. By navigating these dimensions with aptitude and purpose, humans equip themselves to shape a resilient and worthwhile narrative of emotional and psychological nicely-being.

Communicating Effectively

At the heart of boundary mastery lies the paintings of conversation, no longer genuinely approximately sketching traces inside the sand however about expressing those strains in a way that fosters statistics and mutual admire. Declaring obstacles is a bold act of self-expression, a speak that gives clarity to the problematic material of relationships. This system consists of spotting the significance of self-advocacy, a brave act of preserving personal goals without batting an eyelash.

Boundaries stretch in some unspecified time in the future of a massive spectrum, weaving thru numerous factors of human interplay. From the tangible territory of private area to the ethereal limits of emotions, powerful verbal exchange acts because the translator that turns these obstacles right into a shared language of expertise. Communicating physical obstacles entails putting forward preferences concerning touch, non-public space, and privateness. Emotional limitations, at the turn side, require a crafty expression of ways you navigate and percentage your personal feelings and tales.

The paintings of communique in boundary-placing extends beyond spoken phrases to encompass a choreography of non-verbal cues. Verbal articulation calls for using phrases that exactly deliver your goals, expectancies, and obstacles. It's about expressing yourself assertively however with a dash of admire, fostering a talk in which all worried occasions make a contribution to the arrival of a boundary framework that's as sturdy because it is knowing. Non-verbal conversation, encompassing frame language and expressions, performs an further vital function. Harmony among spoken and unstated indicators complements the readability of the communicated limitations.

A keynote inside the symphony of boundary-putting is the virtuoso act of announcing no with grace and firmness. Effective verbal exchange right here includes extra than virtually uttering the word; it's approximately presenting context and rationalization whilst crucial. Saying no turns into a skillful act of balancing commitments, and retaining time and strength for endeavors that align along with your priorities. This issue of conversation prevents misunderstandings and establishes a basis of honesty inner relationships.

Navigating the emotional terrain of boundary-putting requires a deft and powerful talk to maintain your emotional power. Effectively talking emotional limitations includes expressing whilst and the way you prefer to interact in conversations or percentage emotional reviews. It necessitates a clean articulation of your stage of emotional funding in relationships and sports activities activities. This verbal exchange style allows you to guard your mental nicely-being and preserve a enjoy of self amid the complex interplay of interpersonal connections.

In the complex dance of relationships, establishing obstacles is ready crafting a dynamic balance among independence and connection. Effective communication performs a pivotal characteristic in defining dating limitations. This includes brazenly expressing expectations, sharing needs, and respecting the autonomy of all parties concerned. The speak that accompanies dating boundary-putting fosters a shared records that contributes to the formation of relationships which may be collectively supportive, respectful, and conducive to man or woman boom.

The expert landscape goals a one of a kind rhythm in boundary negotiations, wherein powerful conversation takes middle diploma. Clear communication in the place of business includes expressing limits on workload, placing expectations with colleagues, and acknowledging the importance of keeping a healthful paintings-life stability. Articulating professional limitations ensures a transparent understanding among group contributors, contributing to a greater sustainable and effective art work surroundings.

Effective communication is crucial in spotting the fluid nature of limitations. Relationships and activities evolve, requiring you to adjust your limitations in the end. The functionality to talk openly approximately the ones changes includes self-reflected photograph, ongoing talk, and a willingness to comply to the converting dynamics of private and expert connections. This adaptability fosters an surroundings wherein evolving limitations are met with facts and recognize.

Central to powerful conversation in boundary-setting is the cultivation of self-reputation. You have to delve into your triggers, consolation zones, and values to speak obstacles authentically. Self-reputation allows you to articulate your dreams and barriers with readability, fostering an environment wherein others can understand and recognize the ones barriers. It's a journey of introspection that empowers you to talk obstacles that align together with your proper self.

Overcoming guilt associated with putting obstacles is an trouble in which communique takes middle degree. Effective conversation entails expressing the necessity of limitations with out succumbing to guilt. It requires a clean and sincere articulation that setting obstacles is an act of self-care, now not a rejection of others. By correctly talking the reasons in the back of boundary-placing, you navigate the sensitive stability of prioritizing your nicely-being without compromising the relationships spherical you.

Establishing limitations in relationships is a collaborative try that hinges on powerful communique. Creating a culture of understand entails mutual understanding and negotiation of barriers. Effective communication in this context necessitates active listening, open communicate, and a commitment to fostering an environment wherein each human beings enjoy heard, valued, and understood. This collaborative method guarantees that barriers are installation with the shared reason of enhancing the relationship.

In the symphony of boundary-setting, resilience will become a lifelong exercising. Challenges can also upward push up from outside pressures, societal norms, or the evolving nature of relationships. Resilience includes adapting obstacles even as critical, learning from reviews, and final steadfast in prioritizing non-public properly-being.

The artwork of adaptive boundaries lies in balancing flexibility and firmness. Flexibility permits for changes primarily based mostly on evolving times, while firmness guarantees that important values and well-being aren't compromised. It's a sensitive equilibrium that you draw close through self-focus, self-compassion, and an understanding that boundaries are a dynamic element of personal boom.

'

Chapter 15: Strategies For Dealing With Narcissists

Detaching Emotionally

Stumbling upon a narcissist within the tangled jungle of human connections may be a rollercoaster of feelings. Confronting those adorned with narcissistic tendencies wishes a savvy game plan to defend one's emotional sanctuary. At the coronary heart of this approach lies the foxy paintings of emotional detachment—a ninja go with the float to shield in opposition to the complex maneuvers often positioned within the arsenal of narcissistic behavior.

Before diving into those tactical maneuvers, interpreting the narcissistic terrain is project-essential. Narcissists strut with a grandiose swagger, fantasizing about global domination at the equal time as pretty in truth misplacing their empathy. Charm drips from them, drawing unsuspecting souls into their gravitational pull. Yet, under this notable facade lurks a fragility triggering protecting maneuvers—manipulation, insatiable admiration dreams, and a sturdy whiff of entitlement.

Emotional detachment isn't a cold-hearted evasion; it's the superhero cape of self-upkeep. Narcissists banquet on emotional reactions, treating them as playthings to manipulate the emotional puppet show. By mastering emotional detachment, people erect a citadel that shields them from the emotional tempest unleashed via narcissists.

The artwork of emotional detachment kicks off with a savvy coping with of private emotions in reaction to the narcissist's antics. Elevated self-focus is the call of the sport sauce, alerting humans even as their feelings are being toyed with. Committing to a kingdom of Zen in the face of narcissistic provocation transforms human beings into emotional superheroes, responding from a position of inner power in vicinity of impulsive reactions.

A linchpin of emotional detachment is the recognition quo and protection of rock-strong obstacles. Narcissists are boundary pushers, attempting out limits to evaluate how a good deal control they could exercising. Erecting easy and unwavering limitations sends a loud message that manipulative antics are off-limits. It's a shout-out for self-appreciate and a manifesto for private autonomy.

Balancing empathy with emotional detachment requires finesse. Acknowledging the narcissist's struggles with out being weighed down with the useful resource in their emotional bags is an art work. Here, empathy is a device for comprehension, now not an invitation to sign up inside the rollercoaster of their emotional chaos. Navigating interactions with detached empathy is a excessive-wire act.

Detached empathy delves into the origins of narcissistic conduct. Many narcissists wield maladaptive coping mechanisms spawned from past traumas. Understanding this doesn't excuse their antics however offers a lens to preserve emotional detachment. It's a hobby that their movements are regularly a mirrored image of internal turmoil in preference to a remark at the purpose's truly well worth.

In the tango with a narcissist, communication transforms right right into a strategic chess enterprise for emotional detachment. Calm assertiveness turns into the weapon of choice—expressing goals and obstacles with poised readability. This method dodges the emotional bullets narcissists fireside, preventing reactive emotional responses that may be manipulated.

Strategic conversation consists of a dose of thriller. Narcissists thrive on exploiting private records for manipulation. Limiting private disclosure and keeping an air of thriller deprive them of ammunition. It's a tactical flow that fortifies emotional detachment.

The "gray rock" approach, similar to a masterful poker face, is a to be had card to play. Morphing into a bland, unresponsive entity—the grey rock—robs the narcissist of the emotional dinner party they crave. Responding with minimum emotion and turning in non-enticing solutions creates a less worthwhile stage for their manipulative theatrics.

Emotional detachment flourishes on a food plan of sturdy self-care. Narcissistic encounters can drain emotional reserves, making self-care a lifeline for replenishment. Activities that supply delight, rest, and success act as a fortified protection. Whether it's indulging in hobbies, basking inside the business enterprise of supportive comrades, or working towards mindfulness, self-care stands as the fortress in opposition to emotional siege.

Punctuating self-care is the crucial ritual of self-reflected photograph. It provides a location to device feelings, evaluate the effect of narcissistic encounters, and excellent-tune techniques for emotional detachment.

Journaling, healing durations, or moments of serene introspection collect the scaffolding of emotional resilience.

Isolation, a favorite weapon of narcissists, crumbles in the face of a fortified manual network. Trusted confidantes, family allies, or guide companies inject a dose of validation and knowledge. Sharing opinions with empathetic souls reinforces a feel of truth, counteracting the gaslighting the narcissists weave.

Expanding the manual network to encompass professional guidance is a strategic maneuver. Therapists or counselors versed in narcissistic warfare offer profitable insights and coping strategies. Providing a haven for emotional exploration, they contribute to honing the potential of emotional detachment.

In scenarios entailing intense narcissistic abuse, the battleground shifts to jail and protection issues. Emotional detachment extends into sensible picks to defend well-being. Seeking crook counsel, acquiring restraining orders if vital, and fortifying personal safety measures grow to be not actually bodily shields however pillars of a whole technique for emotional detachment.

For the ones entangled with narcissists in co-parenting or familial sagas, more strategies are important. "Parallel parenting," a tactic wherein co-dad and mom disentangle from each different's sagas, emerges as a sly waft. It curtails direct touch, minimizing opportunities for manipulation. In the arena of own family dynamics, implementing wholesome obstacles will become paramount. This might also moreover incorporate proscribing publicity to poisonous family individuals or organising unassailable hints for interaction.

www.ingramcontent.com/pod-product-compliance
Lightning Source LLC
Chambersburg PA
CBHW051728020426
42333CB00014B/1208